SNOWSHOEING

A TRAILSIDE GUIDE
BY
LARRY OLMSTED

A TRAILSIDE SERIES GUIDE

W. W. NORTON & COMPANY

NEW YORK   LONDON

Look for these other Trailside® Series Guides:

Bicycling: Touring and Mountain Bike Basics
Canoeing: A Trailside Guide
Cross-Country Skiing: A Complete Guide
Fly Fishing: A Trailside Guide
Hiking & Backpacking: A Complete Guide
Kayaking: Whitewater and Touring Basics
Parents' Guide to Hiking & Camping: A Trailside Guide
Rock Climbing: A Trailside Guide
Winter Adventure: A Complete Guide to Winter Sports

First Edition

The text of this book is composed in Bodoni Book with the display set in Triplex
Page composition by Eugenie Seidenberg Delaney
Color separations and prepress by Bergman Graphics, Incorporated
Manufacturing by South China Printing Co. Ltd.
Illustrations by Ron Hildebrand

Book design by Bill Harvey

Library of Congress Cataloging-in-Publication Data

Olmsted, Larry, 1966-
Snowshoeing : a trailside guide / by Larry Olmsted.
p.   cm. — (A trailside series guide)
Includes bibliographical references and index.
ISBN 0-393-31720-X
1. Snowshoes and snowshoeing. I. Title. II. Series.
GV853.054   1997   796.92—dc21   97-22846

W. W. Norton & Company, Inc., 500 Fifth Avenue, New York, NY 10110
http://web.wwnorton.com
W. W. Norton & Company Ltd., 10 Coptic Street, London WC1A 1PU

1 2 3 4 5 6 7 8 9 0

CONTENTS

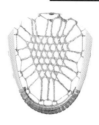

W H Y
S N O W S H O E ?

When you're born, you first learn to crawl, then to walk. For getting into winter sports, snowshoeing is your first few baby steps. From there, you can get into Alpine or Nordic skiing, snowboarding, whatever, or you can just keep snowshoeing.

This is how Andrew Bielecki of Breckenridge, Colorado, explained snowshoeing to me. He should know. Andrew is the country's foremost promoter of snowshoe events and has organized series of races for many of the leading snowshoe manufacturers. His events range from simple 5 kilometer races to combined snowshoe and snowboard events, to his ultimate accomplishment, Extreme

Heat, a desert snowshoe race on sand (see "It's Not Just a Winter Sport," page 14).

A decade ago, Andrew would have had a difficult time finding sponsors and participants for his events. Although snowshoes have been used for winter travel for thousands of years, it was only in the 1800s that they began to be used recreationally, with the organization of early snowshoe clubs. Even then, snowshoes were still used more for practical transportation than for fun, and it is only in the last few years that snowshoeing has become wildly popular as a sport.

Sales of snowshoes have more

Modern snowshoeing knows few bounds: It's for old and young, hikers and racers, walkers and stalkers, even leapers!

popular winter sports, including snowboarding and telemark skiing. Most important, improvements in design and materials have made snowshoes much easier to use, and similar advances in related outdoor gear (such as footwear and clothing) have made winter outdoor activities much more pleasurable.

My favorite reason to snowshoe is the utter simplicity of the sport. Anyone can do it: for a half an hour or a half a week, in the backyard or in the backcountry; without lessons, lift tickets, or even much equipment. It's like taking those first baby steps all over again, only this time in the snow.

THE ORIGINS OF THE SNOWSHOE

Most historians believe that snowshoes were invented between 4,000 and 6,000 years ago. The earliest designs were simply pieces of wood lashed to the user's feet. This basic device demonstrated the principle behind every snowshoe (and ski): that distributing a person's weight over a larger surface area increases flotation, which, in turn, reduces the distance that the person sinks into the snow.

Snowshoes were first developed in central Asia. These early winter travelers then split into two groups; one group continued to use and innovate snowshoes, the other abandoned them. This latter group headed north-

than doubled every year since 1990, making snowshoeing one of the fastest growing winter sports in the United States. The number of snowshoe manufacturers has mushroomed, and there are now more than 20 different widely available brands, up from just a handful at the beginning of 1990.

There are as many reasons for the recent rise in popularity of snowshoeing as there are beautiful winter days (and nights). As a nation, we have become increasingly interested in fitness, nature, and adventure — and snowshoeing involves all three. Snowshoeing, as Andrew quickly realized, also complements other

Snowshoers explore Little Cottonwood Canyon, Wasatch Mountains, Utah. The snowshoe provides an ideal means of absorbing all that winter has to offer without the distractions (and hazards) of skiing.

west into Scandinavia, where it perfected another mode of winter transport — the Nordic ski. The former group used its new invention to migrate through Siberia and over the then-frozen Bering Strait to North America. Snowshoes have been used on this continent ever since these earliest settlers arrived.

Native Americans, especially the Algonquin Indians in the Northeast, raised snowshoe manufacturing from its crude beginnings to a science, and then to an art. The popular theory is that they created their various snowshoe designs based on the feet of animals found in nature who were well suited to winter snow travel.

The design of snowshoes advanced, as a result of difficult weather and terrain conditions.

Inhabitants of the Northeast needed to maneuver through narrow spaces in the dense forests. They developed smaller shoes that achieved this goal, while still supporting their weight on the wet, heavy snow common to this region. In contrast, the deep, light snow of Alaska demanded a much larger shoe for adequate flotation. Snowshoes developed in this region, therefore, were much longer, and thus more difficult to turn. However, this was not a problem, since the ability to maneuver in tight spaces was not an issue as in the Northeast, due to Alaska's open terrain.

Despite the differences in design, snowshoes fulfilled the same important function in all parts of the country above the snowbelt: They allowed users to move over otherwise

Over the centuries the snowshoe has undergone many useful refinements and a few dead ends. 1) The classic Pickerel with hide decking is growing rare; 2) a traditional frame shape with very nontraditional steel wire decking is extinct; 3) the Western is the prototype for many modern shoes; 4) another extinct "innovation;" 5) the bearpaw, granddaddy of modern shoes.

while discovering new routes that were later used during westward expansion, as did the trappers and surveyors who followed in their footsteps. Snowshoes also carried thousands of miners to gold rushes in Alaska and the Yukon territory. Today, these relics hang on cabin walls from Anchorage to Aspen, reminders of the important role that snowshoes played in this country's rich heritage of exploration, expansion, and economic growth.

impassable terrain, thus enabling them to participate in activities that were vital to survival, such as hunting and food gathering. Additionally, early European settlers in North America engaged in other pursuits that also benefited from the use of snowshoes. French Canadian fur traders could not have successfully plied their trade without snowshoes. This industry became an indispensable part of the Northeast's economy, and the backbone of early commercial efforts like the Hudson Bay Company, one of the first of the large conglomerates on this continent.

Explorers used snowshoes

Born of necessity, snowshoeing later became a recreational activity as well, and there have been several "rebirths" in the popularity of the sport, although none as profound as the one occurring today. Two hundred years ago, residents of Quebec formed snowshoe clubs, complete with elaborate costumes and music. They held hikes and races, often coupling snowshoeing with eating and drinking — particularly the latter.

Solitude and a sunset, Mount Rainier, Washington. For many, this is snowshoeing's ultimate reward.

On snowshoes you will discover a world of winter hiking, whether in groups, solo, or with a canine companion.

continued into the 1930s, but interest waned when another new winter sport, Alpine skiing, arrived on the scene. After World War II, many of this country's largest ski resorts were opened, and for several decades skiing enjoyed continued growth, while snowshoeing took a back seat.

It seems we have finally come full circle, and snowshoeing is back again with a vengeance. Sales are soaring, and many new snowshoe man-

In the roaring 20s, outing clubs in New England organized events, often called "tramps," throughout the White and Green mountains of Vermont and New Hampshire. Recreational snowshoeing became a popular social event, because anyone could participate. Snowshoe fever

ufacturers have introduced innovative products to the market. The number of snowshoe races held each year has also dramatically increased, and these events can now be found almost anywhere in snow country. Although technology has played a significant part in the latest growth of the sport,

Green Mountain Club outting, Balton Lodge, Long Trail, Vermont, February 22, 1929. These enthusiasts were part of a surge in the popularity of in snowshoeing that ebbed in the 30s when Alpine skiing was "discovered."

the fundamental reasons why people snowshoe have remained the same — it's easy, inexpensive, and lots of fun.

WHY SHOULD I SNOWSHOE?

We reached Taft Lodge before dark; in time to change, make dinner, and enjoy the sunset. My friend Todd Alexander and I had the place to ourselves, which is quite unusual. Located on the backside of Stowe's Mount Mansfield, Taft is one of the most popular lodges on Vermont's Long Trail, a hiking path that runs the length of the state. In the summer, it is often difficult to get a bunk in the lodge, and inconceivable to be alone. However, it was not summer.

It was the middle of January, in the middle of the week. The sun was bright, but the mercury never even attempted to rise above freezing. The person from the Green Mountain Club laughed when I asked if the lodge would be crowded. On our ascent, we first noticed the hard-to-miss tracks of winter hikers. The deep foot-sized marks — "post-holes" — were left by hikers who had sunk up to their knees or thighs in the snow, due to the weight of their bodies. The tracks had ended

The snowshoe's traditional role: a practical, reliable mode of winter transport for outdoorsmen.

abruptly. Apparently, exhaustion had forced these hikers to turn back.

From that point on, the only other evidence of recent activity was a single, rapidly fading pair of cross-country ski tracks that appeared to be at least a day old. They too stopped short of the cabin, and we never saw the skier.

■

Hiking has become extremely popular in recent years — I enjoy it myself. But if escaping civilization is your goal, it is becoming much more difficult to do so in the summer, when popular routes like the Long Trail, Appalachian Trail, and Pacific Crest

GEAR TALK

AS SNOWSHOEING GROWS, SNOWSHOES SHRINK

Early snowshoes were huge by today's standards, with the biggest models reaching over seven feet in length. These models — known as Pickerels, Yukons, Arctics, or Alaskas — were developed for fast travel across wide, open spaces. Today's traditional wooden models can still exceed five feet, but the most popular snowshoes today are made of aluminum, and rarely exceed three feet in length. The all-plastic models are the latest development; some are less than two feet long — a mere quarter of the size of the earliest shoes! In addition to the smaller sizes, modern snowshoes are also made with solid surfaces that offer more flotation per square inch than the older laced styles, which had as much empty space as decking in the webbing.

Trail are jammed with hikers. Despite the growth in popularity of snowshoeing, however, this problem does not yet exist.

That empty cabin represents one of the main attractions of snowshoeing — solitude. But solitude is just one reason why snowshoeing in winter is so enjoyable. Beauty is another. Snow has a way of making everything pristine. In addition, many animals are more likely

Small, lightweight modern snowshoes redefine the sport, making running, racing, and invigorating workouts possible.

to show themselves in winter, because they are not constantly frightened by the presence of humans. There is no better time to commune with nature. And if you have ever experienced black fly season, you can appreciate one of the most underrated reasons for venturing outdoors in winter: there are no bugs. This fact alone is enough to get me out the door, and onto a pair of snowshoes.

But even if hiking the high peaks

and escaping bugs are not on your list of priorities, snowshoeing should be. I participate in just about every winter sport, and enjoy them all. However, if I had to choose just one, it would be snowshoeing, for a variety of reasons.

IT'S AS EASY AS WALKING Sure, there are some advanced techniques to learn (especially for snowshoeing on steep hills and in the backcountry), but mastering a golf course on snow-

IT'S NOT JUST A WINTER SPORT

There's an adage about a salesman so good at his trade that he "could sell ice to an Eskimo." Race promoter Andrew Bielecki of Breckenridge, Colorado has gone one better by selling snowshoes in the desert. Well, not exactly, but for the last two years his Extreme Heat and Extreme Heat 2 races have been hits, and are certainly the only races of their kind in the country. The catch? Competitors strap on their snowshoes and run a hilly five kilometers, not through the snow-covered passes of the Rockies, but through the sand of the Great Sand Dunes National Monument near Alamosa, Colorado, in blistering heat. An eternal optimist, Andrew claims that snowshoes "work even better on sand then snow," and hopes to bring his race to his former home, Hawaii.

shoes will take you only a matter of minutes, particularly with modern shoes. The learning curve is short, and you don't need months, or even hours, of lessons.

YOU CAN SNOWSHOE ANYWHERE THERE IS SNOW (OR SAND) No four-hour drives to ski areas, no $50 lift tickets. Any park, golf course, or wilderness area will do — even a snow-covered parking lot. When winter blizzards hit, city streets and sidewalks can be used for snowshoeing. Snowshoers are also able to ascend trails that are too steep for skiers, and do not need groomed trails to enjoy their sport.

THERE IS LITTLE PREPARATION NEEDED FOR CASUAL SNOWSHOEING You can keep a pair of snowshoes in the trunk of your car and any time you decide to go, you can be on the trail within minutes. No rental lockers, huge duffel bags, or waiting in line.

IT'S A GREAT WORKOUT No matter what your level of fitness, you can participate in snowshoeing. It's a whole-body, low-impact, aerobic activity, and a terrific way to tone up, burn fat, and set an excellent cardio-vascular workout. Many of my friends have become converts and now choose snowshoeing over cross-country skiing as their winter fitness activity.

THERE ARE MANY PLACES THAT SIMPLY CANNOT BE REACHED IN WINTER WITHOUT SNOWSHOES This pertains not only to "basic" snowshoers, but to

TRACKING

One of the biggest attractions of snowshoeing is the solitude it affords. The winter woods are uncrowded, and despite the sudden growth in the sport, on most days you will have the trail to yourself. This means that you are likely to see wildlife; if you do not, the snow makes it possible to observe evidence of recent animal activity.

Animal tracks are the most obvious indication of activity. Using a good field guide to wildlife in your region (e.g.,

Tracking and the Art of Seeing by Paul Rezendes), you can learn to identify various tracks. This is not as easy as it sounds, since the tracks left in the snow rarely match up to the picture-perfect marks depicted in your book.

There are other clues you can use when trying to identify animals. Scat, when paired with tracks, can often help you pin down the depositor. Feeding activities of particular animals can also be of assistance in identification.

Another set of tracks you can

continued on page 16

TRACKING

continued from page 15

identify during your hike is that of other snowshoers. While this has less appeal to the naturalist, snowshoe aficionados may delight in their ability to identify various brands and styles of snowshoes. Classic wooden shoes offer the most distinctive prints, as their webbing leaves a recognizable pattern in the snow.

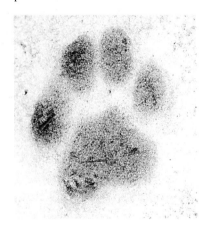

While tracking animals or seeking them out to photograph, be aware that there are a few you do not want to encounter. The odds of this occurring are low, but discretion is the best strategy. If you pull out your handy field guide and identify bear tracks, you would be well served not to follow them. Even in areas that are free of dangerous predators, animals can react erratically, especially if you inadvertently threaten them, so always use caution when tracking wild animals.

One other danger of tracking is simply getting lost. If you become enamored of a particular set of tracks you encounter along the trail, and follow them into the woods, you may forget about time and distance. If this occurs, the simplest solution is to retrace your own steps, following the telltale snowshoe marks you have left behind.

those who mix snowshoeing with other winter sports. My friend Todd, who accompanied me on the Long Trail, is a snowboarding instructor, and first donned snowshoes back in 1986 in Steamboat Springs, Colorado to climb Rabbit Ears Pass with his snowboard: "At the time, a lot of ski areas were banning snowboarders, and there were all these backcountry bowls waiting to be boarded. The problem was getting up [to them]. A lot of the locals discovered snowshoeing then, and we learned that you could [get to these areas by snowshoe, and] board as much as you wanted without ever buying a lift ticket. Today, I just snowshoe for the sake of snowshoeing."

IT'S INEXPENSIVE A cheap pair of

Mount Rainier winter expedition. At a basic level, snowshoes prove their worth as versatile winter hiking boots, allowing mountaineers to overcome backcountry challenges.

SNOWSHOE FESTIVALS: TRY THEM, YOU'LL LIKE THEM

Many skeptics have been convinced of the sport's appeal the first time they strap on a pair of snowshoes, go for a walk, and discover how easy modern snowshoes are to use. To encourage this, many outing clubs and ski resorts — in conjunction with snowshoe manufacturers — offer festivals or "demo-days," where shoes, instruction, and trails are provided at no charge or for a minimal fee. Many of these events offer guided naturalist hikes; others provide lectures on topics such as clothing and winter camping. Instructors are also on hand to help you figure out which type of shoe is right for you. Tubbs Snowshoes has been known to put on snowshoe volleyball matches, and most festivals include a race or two. Not only do these festivals provide ample opportunity for fun, they are also a great way to become acquainted with the sport of snowshoeing. (See Sources & Resources for a list of organizations and manufacturers who put on events.)

With lightweight snowshoes, competitors need not hang up their running shoes until spring.

WHO ELSE WANTS TO SNOWSHOE?

Snowshoeing knows no bounds. The growing popularity of the sport is based on the fact that there is some aspect that appeals to just about everyone:

HIKERS AND MOUNTAINEERS At the most basic level, snowshoes are simply winter hiking boots. For avid hikers, the season never has to end. The same trails that are enjoyed in the summer can also be explored in the winter. Dayhikes or backpacking trips are possible even in the deepest snow, and you can reach your favorite summits by just strapping on a pair of snowshoes. Summit expeditions in high mountains encounter every type of backcountry challenge, from ice climbing and technical rock climbing to hiking and snowfield crossings. On trips such as these, a pair of snowshoes can be a convenience, and more and more expeditions are considering them standard equipment.

SNOWBOARDERS 'Boarders have taken to snowshoes like fish to water, and for good reason. Virgin backcountry bowls are waiting, and snowshoes make getting to them possible. This aspect of the sport has become so popular that snowshoe manufacturers are fitting shoes with the same step-in bindings that are used as snowboards, so you don't have to carry a second pair of boots. Also, consider that four or five days of boarding without having to buy a lift ticket will pay for a nice pair of

snowshoes costs under a hundred dollars. An expensive pair costs less than three hundred. Either will last a lifetime. Some will last for generations. Other necessary gear includes boots and warm winter clothes. There are also some additional items that are handy (but not necessary) to own, such as ski poles and traction aids. (Equipment and accessories will be discussed further in Chapters 2 and 3.)

snowshoes. Not a bad deal.

SKIERS Snowshoes are also available with a variety of Nordic and Telemark bindings, which allow for transfers that are quick and easy. Backcountry skiers are finding that for lengthy climbs, switching to snowshoes beats putting climbing skins on their skis, hands down. For backcountry travel, a snowshoe can also function as a backup to be used if a ski gets broken. With some of today's ultralight or folding snowshoes, carrying a pair strapped to your pack is a logical choice on any backcountry trip.

RUNNERS Nobody's exercise routine suffers more in winter than the runner's. Many avid joggers are forced to hang up their running shoes until spring, or substitute a treadmill at the gym for the great outdoors.

THE EARLY DAYS OF SNOWBOARDING

Snowboarders were among the first to discover the snowshoe renaissance and use it to their advantage. In the early days of snowboarding, when it had a reputation as an "outlaw" sport, many ski resorts forbade snowboarders from riding the lifts. In the Rocky Mountain states, snowboarders responded by donning snowshoes and heading for the hills, where they could board down untracked runs and high, untouched bowls. The snowshoes were their lift tickets — a much less expensive alternative.

When Todd Alexander strapped on his first pair of snowshoes nearly 10 years ago, his perception of winter sports changed forever. Now a snowboard instructor at Vermont's Mount Ascutney Ski Resort, Todd was living in Steamboat Springs, Colorado, and was trying out snowshoes as a way to reach the backcountry off Rabbit Ears Pass for a day of 'boarding.

"Back then snowshoes were an essential part of the snowboard experience, because so many mountains banned 'boarders," he recalls. "Today it's still an alternative to lifts, but now I snowshoe just for the sake of snowshoeing."

Just as skiers still hike up New Hampshire's Tuckerman's Ravine each spring for a quick run down, snowboarders will always find rewards in virgin backcountry routes no matter how many ski resorts embrace their sport. The labor of the climb on snowshoes and the unique descent on a snowboard combine to create a well-rounded day of fun and exercise.

This is why sales of specialty running models are one of the fastest-growing segments of the snowshoe market. Small and light, many of them allow runners to wear their regular sneakers; and snowshoe running offers exercise benefits equal to or greater than road running. I often use my heart rate monitor while training, and find it is easier and faster to reach and maintain my target heart rate during snowshoe running than during regular road running. Soft snow also lessens impact-related strain on the shins and knees. For competitive runners, there are snowshoe races of various lengths held all over the country.

FAMILIES No winter sport is easier to learn than snowshoeing, and the whole family can enjoy it together. Many companies make inexpensive, smaller models for children, and since a pair of snowshoes can be used for a wide weight range, they do not become obsolete each season as your child grows. For full-family participation, snowshoeing is a perfect choice.

I am a snowshoe junkie, and participate in the sport for all of the above reasons. The main one, however, is that it gets me outdoors in the winter. It is worth repeating that snowshoeing is basically walking — and who doesn't like to go for a stroll every now and then? This is especially true when the winter blues set in and cabin fever develops. No matter where you live, no matter how bitter the winters, there will be days when the sun shines and the snow glistens, beckoning you outdoors. Even if you can count these days on one hand, you can depend on them occurring every winter, year after year, and you can respond by strapping on a pair of snowshoes and journeying out into nature.

THE SHOES
FOR YOU

Regardless of the names that manufacturers choose, most modern snowshoes fall into three categories: mountaineering, recreational, and sport.

Mountaineering snowshoes are also called backcountry, backpacking, or hiking shoes. These shoes are for use on the most demanding of terrains — including steep slopes and ice — where good traction, durability, and maneuverability are a necessity. They have sophisticated bindings, and large cleats on the bottom. They also cost the most, because they are made of more expensive materials.

Recreational shoes are also called walking or hiking shoes. They are scaled-down models of mountaineering snowshoes, with less sophisticated bindings, less aggressive traction, and less ability to tolerate the high "levels of abuse" that occur during use in extreme conditions. However, recreational snowshoes are more than adequate for most terrains.

Sport snowshoes are also called running, racing, or cross-training shoes. Some are just lighter versions of recreational models and can be used for hiking. Others are highly specialized, smaller racing models designed for running races — such as 10-Ks — on packed snow. While

Three snowshoe types (from left): modern aluminum-frame solid-deck mountaineering model, wood-frame lace-deck recreational shoe, and asymmetrical sport shoe.

mountaineering models can certainly be used for a walk in the park. Lighter men and women can often use running models for recreational hikes. I know a 115-pound woman who uses a highly specialized running model for all types of snowshoeing.

In general, if you are planning to spend a large amount of time in the backcountry, or enjoy challenging mountain hikes, your best bet is to buy mountaineering shoes. If you are planning to walk flat trails in the park in your neighborhood, and may even go winter camping in the future, choose recreational snowshoes. Running models are often a person's second pair of snowshoes, but if you are a dedicated road runner looking to train in the off-season and don't plan to do much hiking, these lightweight shoes would be ideal for your first pair of snowshoes.

most recreational and mountaineering snowshoes are symmetrical (that is, the left and right foot are identical), many sport models are asymmetrical, with the bindings mounted closer to the inside edge. This enables you to take a more natural stride without having to worry about the inside edges of the shoes hitting each other.

When choosing a pair of snowshoes, you will need to determine which of the three types best suits your needs. This should not be difficult. Do not feel limited by the definitions, since there is a lot of overlap between the three snowshoe categories. Most recreational models can be used in the backcountry, and

SIZE MATTERS

Size is one of the two most important characteristics you will have to decide on before buying snowshoes. The perfect shoe is the smallest one you can get away with — big enough to support your weight, but no bigger. The smaller the shoe, the more maneuverable it is, and the easier it is to walk in. However, flotation is what matters most, since sinking into the snow will seriously compromise your maneuverability. Therefore, it is better to err on the side of too big than too small. A larger shoe may mean a slight increase in weight, and a slight decrease in efficiency, but too small a shoe just won't work. You will sink like a stone.

Two factors affect flotation, and thus determine the size of shoe you will need. The first of these is the amount of weight to be supported. Remember that you need to consider not only your own weight, but the weight of whatever else you will have with you, from socks to candy bars, poles to tents. Full-winter camping gear can easily add 70 or more pounds, so make sure you take into account the type of snowshoeing you will be doing, and the gear that you may need to bring along with you.

The second and more important factor to consider is the type of snow on which you will be snowshoeing. In different parts of the country, the water content of snow varies greatly. The wetter the snow, the denser and heavier it is, and the more weight it

WEST IS WEST, AND EAST IS EAST — SOMETIMES

While some parts of the country tend to get one type of snow more than others, many areas are subject to a variety of conditions. In Colorado for instance, "western" snow, or light powder, and "eastern" snow, which is wetter and heavier, are both common.

Tom Sobal, the nation's most successful snowshoe racer, asks "what is the West anyway? Is it the Sierra Nevada or Utah? It's a gross overgeneralization to say any place gets a certain type of snow."

While he has a point, local norms exist, and when shopping for snowshoes, you should consider what conditions you are most likely to encounter, even though you won't find these conditions every time you go out.

Tom Sobal, the nation's most successful snowshoe racer.

Wet, dense snow supports far more weight. In areas of the country such as the Northeast where such snow is common, you may use smaller snowshoes.

The dryer the snow, the bigger the shoe you'll need. Dry powder, generally found in the Rocky Mountain states, requires the biggest shoes, and even then, you'll sink considerably.

will support. Conversely, light, dry snow supports much less weight. I know of one popular snowshoe model that is rated for 190 pounds in packed snow, but only up to about 145 pounds in dry powder — a significant difference.

The dryer the snow, the bigger the shoe you will need. In truly dry, fresh, deep powder — the finest of which is found in the Wasatch Mountains of Utah — no shoe will support you well, and you will have to concede to sinking and, thus, losing some speed.

You cannot buy one pair of shoes

that is perfect for every snow condition you may encounter. Even if you could, snow conditions can change by the day or by the hour. Sizing snowshoes is an inexact science, so "close enough" is okay. The best rule to follow, is to buy snowshoes based on the type of snow that is most common in the area in which you plan to snowshoe. The three main types of snow are:

DRY POWDER Also called western snow, dry powder is generally found throughout the Rocky Mountain states — especially in Utah — and requires the biggest shoe.

WET SNOW Common in the Northeast, and in coastal regions such as California and the Pacific Northwest, as well as the Sierra Nevada, this type of snow has much more water content and requires a smaller shoe.

GROOMED OR PACKED SNOW Trails are often groomed for snowshoe running races, enabling competitors to wear tiny shoes. Snow can also pack down by itself, under a variety of natural conditions. As with wet snow, a smaller snowshoe can be used on packed snow.

"But I only want to buy one pair of snowshoes," you say. This is understandable. Again, perfect flotation is a luxury, not a necessity. In fact, if you climb a large mountain you will discover that your snowshoe needs change along the way, so there really is no "perfect" size. Buy the smallest shoe that will handle both the most common snow conditions that you'll encounter and the weight you will carry most of time. Don't worry about the exceptions — you can always make do.

SNOW HAS A MIND OF ITS OWN

Falling snow has widely varying characteristics based on moisture content. In addition, many changes occur once snow lands on the ground. Savvy skiers rise at daybreak to hit the slopes after a new "dump" of powder, not only to beat other skiers, but time and Mother Nature, as well. They know that gravity pulls the snow toward the earth, compacting it and making it denser. Even in the untouched wilderness, powder becomes denser over time.

Wind also plays an important role in packing the snow down and making it denser. In fact, in open, windswept areas, wind-packed snow can become so dense that Eskimos are able to cut blocks out of it and use them to build igloos.

Warmer temperatures generally make for firmer snow: the snow melts during the day and refreezes at night, becoming denser. On the other hand, snow in very cold, windless regions — like the forests of Minnesota, where the temperatures remain well below zero for weeks on end — will remain light.

Denser snow is better for snowshoeing, so welcome the sun, the wind, and time. If you are out West and get a big powder storm and find yourself unable to effectively move around on your snowshoes, just wait until it firms up a bit. This may take a few hours or a few days, depending on the conditions.

Snowshoe manufacturers love to include dimensions in their shoe descriptions — 9" x 29", 10" x 36", 12" x 34", and so on. The reason that they include these measurements is to allow buyers to estimate the surface areas (and thus, compare the flotation) of differently shaped shoes easily, when visual comparisons are difficult — for example, between a nearly round shoe and a long, slim oval. Don't bother. The age-old formulas for choosing the right snowshoe size based on weight and square inches can no longer be trusted, since modern materials and designs have affected the flotation of differently shaped shoes. Due to these differences in flotation from model to model, any attempt to compare one pair of snowshoes to another based on surface area would be like trying to compare apples to oranges.

Most manufacturers offer a recommended weight rating for their shoes. Usually a tag on the shoes will state what weight range the model is designed to support. You can use this

WINTER WEIGHT GAIN

When studying the weight ratings on snowshoes, don't forget the extra weight you will be carrying in the winter. Most people weigh themselves while naked on a bathroom scale, but only a fool would go snowshoeing au naturel. Forget about vanity — for a good estimate you'll need to consider not only your true weight, but the weight of your clothing and other gear as well. Depending on where you are going and how long you'll be there, you might end up carrying quite a heavy load. For example:

SHORT GOLF COURSE OUTING (BASIC GEAR)
- Boots
- Pants
- Shirt
- Shell
- Gloves
- Poles
- Hat

10 to 13 pounds

DAYHIKE
- Basic gear (above)
- Pack
- Water
- Snacks
- Extra layer of clothes
- First aid/repair kit
- Map
- Compass
- Filter
- Matches

20 to 28 pounds

information to compare various brands. A few manufacturers include snow conditions on their fitting charts, but many do not. Since it is more important to know the type of snow the shoes are designed for than their weight rating, look at where the shoes are made. A manufacturer in Salt Lake City who rates a shoe for 200 pounds most likely has something different in mind than one from Vermont, since these regions have very different snow conditions and therefore different flotation requirements.

WOOD: THE CLASSIC SNOWSHOE

Since snowshoe designs have changed considerably with the introduction of newer materials, it is easiest to classify snowshoes according to the material they are made of, as opposed to their design. Therefore, all wooden shoes are classified as "traditional," and all shoes made of materials other than wood are classified as "modern," even though new, more advanced designs of wooden shoes continue to be manufactured to this day.

OVERNIGHT EXCURSION
- Basic gear (above)
- Pack
- Food
- Water
- Stove
- Pots
- Sleeping bag
- Tent
- Additional clothing
- Map
- Global Positioning System receiver
- First aid/repair kit
- Camp clothes
- Miscellaneous items

50 to 75 pounds or more

The best way to pick the right snowshoe is to try before you buy. Most snowshoe events, such as races or festivals, offer demonstration pairs. Many Nordic ski areas now rent snowshoes and offer lessons, as well. There are also sporting goods stores (including major outdoor recreation chains like EMS and REI) that rent snowshoes. These retailers can be found in most winter resort towns, and some even have programs where the rental fees can be applied toward your eventual purchase. (Some shops go so far as to offer a satisfaction guarantee that allows you to exchange your purchase for credit toward another pair of snowshoes within a certain period of time if you are dissatisfied.)

A traditional Green Mountain style shoe with raw cowhide decking and modern binding.

in forested land, and shorter individuals may find them unwieldy.

THE MAINE OR MICHIGAN shoe is also known as the Beavertail. These are large shoes in both width and length, although they are not as long as those in the Pickerel family. As the name implies, Beavertails have tails that are intended to drag. This helps these larger shoes to track in a straight line. They are suited to travel in deep snow, but are difficult to handle, and, therefore, are a poor choice for wooded or hilly regions.

THE BEARPAW is the most common snowshoe design. Bearpaws are oval — sometimes nearly round. There are several variations of the Bearpaw. The original style was round and flat, with no tail or upturned toe. These models provided only fair flotation, but excellent maneuverability. Original Bearpaws were often used in hilly country, where the flat toes had a tendency to dig into the snow on descents, catching snowshoers unaware and tripping them up. This problem led to the innovation of the upturned toe, which is now the standard on most snowshoes.

"MODIFIED BEARPAWS" have narrower heels, in addition to upturned toes. A Bearpaw snowshoe with a tail is sometimes referred to as a BEAVERTAIL. This is unfortunate, as it causes much confusion with the Maine/Michigan snowshoe.

The final style of Bearpaw, also known as the WESTERN, is the Green

Styles

Among traditional models there are three or four basic styles, which go by different names in different regions.

THE PICKEREL, also called the Yukon, Alaska, Arctic, Trail, or Cross-Country, is a long (up to five feet) narrow snowshoe with a tail. These are fast shoes, intended for rapid travel across open country in light, dry snow. Because of their length, they are difficult to maneuver

Mountain model. This shoe is nearly oval in shape, with a slightly tapered heel and an upturned toe, and is the basis of most "modern" snowshoe designs.

With traditional snowshoes, it is important that you pick the design based on the terrain and snow conditions in your area. Your choice will depend on which qualities you most value: flotation, maneuverability, or the ability to climb and descend. You should also select shoes based on your level of experience, as some of the larger shoes are more difficult to use and, therefore, a poor choice for novices. A modification of the Bearpaw is probably the easiest wooden snowshoe to master, and is also the model most suited to a wide variety of snow conditions and terrains.

Materials

Until the 1980s, your choice of snowshoe frame material was limited almost entirely to wood. Economical wooden frames were made of maple, but the best material in terms of durability was — and still is — white ash. Today, most frames on wooden shoes are made of white ash.

A hotly contested issue among wooden shoe connoisseurs is the type of decking material used. The original material of choice was raw cowhide, which, after being laced into the desired pattern, was wet down and then allowed to dry so that it would shrink to fit the frame tightly. The drawback with this material is that it stretches and sags when wet, and is then more likely to tear. This generally occurs only at temperatures above freezing, when the snow is moist and soaks the lacing.

In order to overcome this problem, manufacturers began using neoprene as a decking material. Neoprene is a nylon-based synthetic material that does not stretch or sag. However, it is not as resistant to abrasion at colder temperatures as is rawhide. The choice of lacing is one of personal preference, but rawhide is generally favored in regions that experience consistently cold temperatures.

Whichever material you choose, be aware that wooden shoes require regular maintenance, while most "modern" shoes do not. They also need to be stored carefully when not in use (see "Care and Maintenance of Your Wooden Shoes," opposite).

Bindings

Most wooden shoes take one of two binding designs. Early manufacturers developed the H binding, consisting of a strap around the heel crossed by a strap at the toe and one at the instep, forming an "H." Variations of this design are still used on many traditional snowshoes. A more modern alternative is based on a binding design pioneered by the Sherpa Snowshoe Company, which is used on their aluminum snowshoes, as well. This binding utilizes a shoelace and hooks like those on a hiking boot to draw material up and around the foot. It is easy to take on and off and adjust.

Wooden shoes are often sold without bindings — you purchase them separately and then attach them. Therefore, it's important to make sure that your snowshoes and bindings are compatible when you buy them.

Tubbs, the country's largest snowshoe manufacturer, has applied some of their modern innovations to the traditional shoe. By inserting a metal pivot rod into their Select Grade wooden shoes, they are able to mount the same high-tech binding that is used on their aluminum models. Unlike conventional wooden shoe bindings, these high-tech bindings are not secured to the decking, and, therefore, allow for the attachment of cleats under the toes, where they are most effective in providing traction.

WOOD I?

There are still mass producers and custom craftsmen who make traditional snowshoes, and many veteran snowshoers will use nothing but wooden shoes. However, it is no coincidence that snowshoeing has become more popular since the introduction of the modern shoe, which many believe is easier to use. So the big question is: Why buy a wooden model?

There is no doubt that wooden shoes work well, and if properly cared for, can last a lifetime. But the frames can also be broken on rocks, and damage in the field is harder to repair on traditional models than on modern models.

Wooden shoes do, however, have two distinct advantages over modern shoes. First, they are generally less expensive than modern shoes of comparable quality. Some companies even sell their frames and lacing separately as a kit, allowing you the pleasure of building your own shoes. This not only saves more money, but gives you the satisfaction of tra-

versing winter landscapes on your own handiwork (see "Making Your Own Shoes," page 33).

Wooden shoes are also classics, and are simply more elegant in both design and appearance than modern shoes. Since the vast majority of snowshoes now being sold are modern models, showing up for a snowshoe outing in a traditional pair will often make you the center of attention. This is particularly true if you invest in a handmade pair from an expert snowshoe maker (see Sources & Resources for a list of custom snowshoe makers).

Form versus function is a heated debate in every outdoor sport, and snowshoeing is no exception. For many individuals, the modern shoe is a better choice than the traditional shoe. But if aesthetics are important to you, consider a traditional pair.

An advantage of snowshoes over skis is the stability and maneuverability they offer, a boon to young families

CARE AND MAINTENANCE OF YOUR WOODEN SHOES

At the end of winter, you will need to prepare your wooden snowshoes for a season of inactivity. This means recoating the frames with clear varnish or shellac — two coats if possible. If you have rawhide lacings, they should also be coated. With neoprene, care should be taken not to coat the laces, which can be difficult. Depending on the type of bindings you have, especially if they are leather, the manufacturer may recommend applying a coat of wax. You will have to remove the bindings to do this and to adequately varnish the lacings. Finally, store your snowshoes in a cool, dry place, away from sharp objects and animals. They seem to make an especially tasty treat for rodents.

After all, no one is going to hang a pair of neon-colored aluminum shoes on the wall of a cabin.

THE MODERN SNOWSHOE

Most modern snowshoe frames are made of aluminum. The most popular design is an aluminum frame in an oval shape, similar to the Green Mountain Bearpaw or Western shoe, but with a solid synthetic deck rather than lacing. Recently, however, a wide variety of alternative materials, designs, and features have sprung up, including plastic, folding frames, and metal decks. Nonetheless, there is still a basic logic to modern snowshoe design. The key parts, whether separate or integrated (as they are on plastic shoes), are the binding, frame, deck, and traction devices.

GEAR TALK

BUYING SNOWSHOES

The key factors to consider when selecting your snowshoes are flotation (based on your weight and snow conditions), binding design, and how you'll use the shoes. As far as use, begin by narrowing your search to models designed for activities you are interested in, such as backcountry mountaineering or running.

Just trying on snowshoes in a shop will not allow you to determine whether or not you will be happy with their performance. A short walk around a snow-covered parking lot, although not an ideal test, is better than nothing. There are several things to look for when testing out snowshoes. First, make sure the shoes support your weight. They will sink a little, but should not sink more than six to eight inches; slightly more in dry powder. It should be easy to lift each shoe out of the snow after each step. If they appear to be the right size for you, try them while holding something heavy — to represent a load of gear — and make sure they still support you.

Undo the bindings and remove the shoes. Then put them back on again while you are still outside. If your fingers are falling off from frostbite by the time you get them adjusted, they may be too difficult to use. You will have to occasionally adjust your bindings while snowshoeing, so make sure you can do this easily. Shake your feet violently to see whether the bindings loosen or have any side-to-side play. Properly fitted snowshoes should remain snug and closely follow the movement of your foot.

Bindings

Bindings are the heart and soul of the modern snowshoe. In fact, advances in binding technology were largely responsible for the recent resurgence in snowshoeing. Better bindings make snowshoes much easier to use, improve traction, increase maneuverability and lateral control, and enable a more efficient transfer of energy. Traditional bindings have a lot of slop: between foot and binding, and binding and shoe. A more precise fit means that less energy is exerted by the snowshoer on each step.

All manufacturers have developed proprietary binding devices — each claiming distinct advantages over the others. Atlas uses a patented "spring-loaded" binding, which they say raises the toe with every step. Sherpa, the acknowledged pioneer in modern binding design, claims their "dual rotation system" works well in all types of conditions. All modern bindings are developed based on the

MAKING YOUR OWN SHOES

In addition to the financial savings, there is a certain pride experienced when traversing winter snows on shoes you've built by hand. Some outdoor centers or outing clubs offer classes in snowshoe design and construction. A simpler option is to order snowshoes in kit form.

Making the frames is the hardest part, and this is where kits have a distinct advantage (see Sources & Resources for information regarding where to purchase snowshoe kits). Usually the frames come assembled; at the very least, the exterior of the frame is bent. If you are making them from scratch, you will need an elaborate steaming device to bend the wood — preferably white ash — into shape, as well as some jigs and clamps to hold it in place while it dries. Even for experienced craftsmen with specialized equipment, breakage is common during this process.

Lacing is the "fun" part of construction, and although challenging, does not require the equipment or skill needed to make the frames. Kits usually come with a lacing diagram and instructions. If you are not using a kit, you can obtain literature describing this process from an outing club, or attempt to duplicate the pattern of an existing shoe. To finish making your snowshoes, you will need to varnish the frames and laces. Then your labor of love will be ready for use.

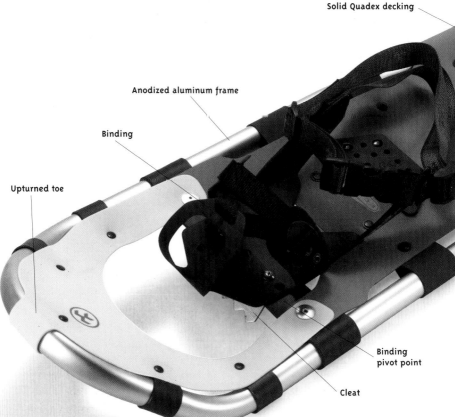

Solid Quadex decking

Anodized aluminum frame

Binding

Upturned toe

Binding
pivot point

Cleat

recognition that the pivoting action of the foot is of utmost importance to snowshoers.

As in cross-country skiing, a snowshoer's heel comes up on every step. Unlike cross-country skiing, hiking, or any other sport, however, the toe also goes down. For this reason, almost every snowshoe has a hole cut out in the decking around the binding. The front of your foot passes through this hole and into the snow, below the surface level of the snowshoe. For this to be possible, the binding must pivot.

There are two basic pivot systems. The first is a pivot rod or bar, a metal rod around which the binding is mounted, allowing a wide range of pivot action. This action is often called free rotation. The other mechanism is a pivot belt or strap, a flat piece of material that pivots by bending, rather than rotating around a fixed rod. This results in "fixed" or "limited" rotation, with less range in pivot. Each system has pros and cons, and different manufacturers

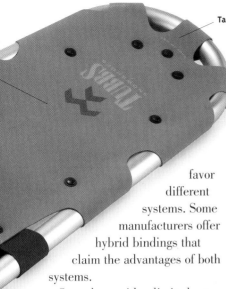

Tail

which assists you when you are breaking trail in fresh powder. You can also get better traction while climbing, because you are able to dig your toe into the slope. Many backcountry and mountaineering models employ free rotation.

Bear in mind that the pivot mechanism will be under a tremendous amount of stress, as it is the only moving part on your snowshoes. Therefore, look for a ruggedly built design. Additional features to look for in a binding are similar to those you would consider when buying any piece of footwear: comfort, fit, and ease of use.

COMFORT Bindings should fit snugly without cutting off your circulation or creating pressure points. If the straps are rubbing or digging into your foot in the store, you will be extremely uncomfortable on the trail.

favor different systems. Some manufacturers offer hybrid bindings that claim the advantages of both systems.

Snowshoes with a limited-rotation binding system lift completely off the ground with every step. This is because the tail can only fall a certain distance. With a free-rotation system the tail tends to drag, since there is unlimited pivot.

Limited rotation reduces energy loss, and is more efficient when used on packed trails. For this reason, almost all racing/running models utilize fixed-rotation systems. However, these tend to have "rebound," which can result in an annoying slapping of the snowshoe against your heel. It is slightly easier to back up with fixed-rotation shoes, although backing up is not something you normally want to do while wearing snowshoes (see Chapter 4).

Free rotation works better in unbroken snow and on steep terrain. While the heel of the shoe falls away with free rotation, the toe also rises,

FIT Snowshoe bindings should fit a wide variety of footwear, since you might also use more than one pair of boots for snowshoeing, depending on the temperature. If you have a large boot size, make sure the bindings will open enough to fit. If you are planning on wearing running shoes — which you might with running snowshoes — make sure the bindings can be tightened enough to fit snugly, so that there is little or no lateral wiggle. If you shake your foot back and forth, the whole snowshoe should follow closely.

EASE OF USE With most modern bindings it is necessary to read the directions before using them. Make

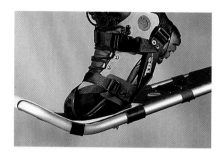

Two binding systems: Limited-rotation bindings (top) reduce energy loss and are most efficient used on packed trails and for running, where having the tail drag would be a drag. Free-rotation bindings (bottom) work better in unbroken snow and on steep terrain. They allow for greater traction while climbing because you can dig your toe into the slope.

sure that once you understand how the binding works, you can put it on and take it off easily. If putting on your snowshoes is a major production, you are less likely to use them. The best bindings are ones that you need to adjust only once, and can then put on again quickly, with as little as one buckle.

The bindings you purchase will determine whether you love or hate your snowshoes. Therefore, put a lot of thought and trial runs into choosing them. I'll say it again: rent before you buy. A binding that feels great in the shop may loosen up on the trail.

Unfortunately, many bindings do this, but it should not be tolerated. Buckles become much harder to negotiate when they are clogged with snow and your gloveless fingers are freezing. In addition, some straps absorb water when warm, then freeze as the temperature drops, becoming rock hard. You do not want to be continually adjusting your bindings on the trail!

Amazingly, many manufacturers seem to design their bindings to be put on in your living room, rather than at a trailhead. When trying on snowshoes, remember that adjustments will, at times, have to be made outside in the snow. I've had a snowshoe come off in midstride many times — not a fun experience. There are some bindings that will remain snug for your entire trip. Settle for nothing less!

Many modern bindings are variations on the H binding; others incorporate entirely new designs. Redfeather's snowshoes feature a pocket made of fabric that surrounds your entire foot. Tubbs's newest top-of-the-line RCS bindings use ratcheting straps similar to those found on Alpine ski boots. Atlas's new Summit series utilizes snowboard-style bindings. A brilliantly simple style is that of Northern Lites, which uses a belt-like design, with holes and hooks.

The goal of all of these designs is to prevent slippage of the straps, which loosens the bindings. I generally avoid bindings that rely on a

Snowshoe runner, San Juan Mountains, Colorado. Her snowshoes are equipped with limited-rotation bindings, and so the tails do not flop down as she lifts her foot to take another stride.

friction buckle through which the strap is passed twice, such as those used on a backpack shoulder strap. In my experience, these tend to loosen up under the considerable amount of motion involved in snowshoeing, and they are difficult to adjust precisely.

One of the simplest, yet most effective bindings is the latest version of the original modern binding introduced by Sherpa. Sherpa uses conventional laces pulled around speed lacing hooks — as on some hiking boots and ice skates — for a binding that laces quickly and easily, fits snugly, and stays put.

A recent innovation worth serious consideration is the step-in binding. It has two metal bands, one at the toe and one at the heel, which lock onto grooves in your boot. This binding is designed to fit like the crampons that are used for ice climbing and mountaineering, and will only work with a boot designed to accommodate crampons. If you have hard-shell mountaineering boots or heavy-duty hikers that can accept crampons, give this binding a try. It is secure, light, and very easy to take on and off. Many manufacturers now offer the step-in as an optional binding on their snowshoes.

1) A mountaineering model with a shape designed for improved stability and ease of walking; 10"x36", 5.6 lbs.
2) An all-around recreational shoe with a broad, round tail for stability and flotation; 9"x30", 4.4 lbs.
3) An asymmetrical sport model; 8"x25", 38 oz.
4) A scaled-down children's shoe; 6.5"x17.5", 1.6 lbs.

EURO-SHOES

With the American snowshoe market maturing, many manufacturers have turned their attention overseas, and modern American snowshoes are now available throughout the world. But until recently, if you shopped for snowshoes in Europe, your only option would be funny-looking, oddly shaped, brightly colored, plastic things. Technique Sport Loisir (TSL) has long been manufacturing these shoes in the French Alps, and the active Europeans who use them are no strangers to winter camping, backcountry skiing, and mountaineering. Now these unique snowshoes are available in the States.

Frames

The frame of a modern snowshoe is usually made of aircraft-grade aluminum. This material comes in sections, and different manufacturers use different techniques to assemble their frames. Atlas's snowshoes are T.I.G.-welded by hand, for instance, a process they claim produces the strongest frames. In general, all aluminum frames are quite durable.

As stated previously, the tail of the traditional wooden snowshoe drags in the snow and helps the shoe to track in a straight line. Since improved binding technology has made snowshoes much more responsive, this feature is not a necessity; however, some modern manufacturers still incorporate a tail, claiming that the tail, in combination with a narrower heel, help to reduce clearance between the shoes, making it less likely that you will step on the inside back edge of your lead shoe. Tails seem to be especially popular with companies — such as Redfeather and Northern Lites — that are known for manufacturing sport models used in running. Tubbs adds tails to their smaller running models, as well.

The majority of hiking and mountaineering frame designs are oval in shape, and almost every

modern snowshoe has an upturned toe, which serves two purposes. It keeps snow from accumulating on the front of the shoe, and it also makes lifting the shoe and moving from one step to the next easier, since the upturned toe is closer to the surface of the snow.

Decking

One of the most important innovations in modern snowshoe design is the development of "solid surface" decking, in which the entire space inside the frame is covered. A traditional shoe is laced with strips, leaving quite a lot of open space in the surface area of the decking. The increased surface area of the solid decking enhances the modern shoe's ability to support more weight than a traditional shoe of the same size. Some claim that the amount of snow that comes through the spaces in the webbing of a traditional shoe is negligible, and thus the flotation difference between solid and laced deckings is minimal. My experience, however,

Modern decking is made of durable synthetics that resist stretching even when wet and cracking even when cold.

Lighter, stronger materials such as aluminum frames and PVC-based solid decking allows for smaller shoes that offer far more freedom of movement.

that are most often nylon or PVC-based. These materials are very durable, and can withstand many years of use. A wide variety of trade-marked materials are used for the decking, including Hypalon, Quadex, Coolthane, and Technitrac. Hypalon, a coated nylon material, is the most common, and used by many manufacturers. Quadex is a more expensive, stronger material found on some high-end models.

One recent introduction to the market has been the all-

has been that small all-plastic shoes are able to carry as much weight as larger, wooden, laced models.

Modern shoe decking is manufactured using synthetic materials

plastic shoe. Plastic models have been manufactured for decades, but they were originally novelty items or children's toys. Only in the last few years have manufacturers developed plastic snowshoes for the general market. Mountain Safety Research makes an expandable model: the front and back overlap and you can adjust the surface area based on the amount of flotation needed. TSL, the leading European snowshoe manufacturer, makes an entire product line of plastic shoes with a variety of binding options. Little Bear Snowshoes, a new company out of Colorado, makes a no-frills injection-molded plastic model so durable that they recommend using them under your car tires for traction if you get stuck in the snow!

Hard plastic models are unique because the frame and decking are one and the same. They are also much less expensive, and often lighter, than aluminum shoes. I have been impressed with TSL's high-tech, hard plastic shoes and use them in the backcountry, where they fit comfortably in a daypack and add very little weight.

Ramer, a company from Colorado, makes a unique snowshoe that is fashioned from a solid piece of aluminum — a metal version of the plastic models. Originally developed for use by the U.S. Army's Special

A new Tubbs model with aluminum frame and one-piece molded polyurethane deck makes for a low-maintenance, reasonably-priced shoe. Note molded traction pattern.

Forces, the manufacturer states that these snow-shoes also make good shovels and stove platforms. The shoe is small and light and can accommodate a wide variety of footwear.

TRACTION SYSTEMS

This is yet another area of snowshoe design that has changed dramatically in recent years. Once upon a time, I would have entitled this section "crampons," but that term does not cover the wide variety of traction aids available today.

Ironically, modern aluminum snowshoes need traction aids more than traditional ones. Since the solid decking surfaces and aluminum frames are smooth and slippery it is impossible to climb even a moderate grade with most modern shoes, whereas the rough lacing of a traditional shoe provides some built-in traction. Slide your hand across the surface of a tennis racket and a dinner plate and you will understand the comparison. Although not as essential, many snowshoers attach traction aids to traditional shoes, also.

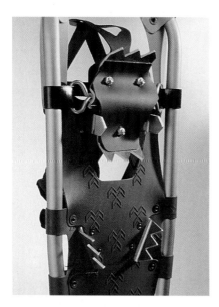

Traction comes in several forms, including (above) toe- and heel-mounted steel cleats and (right) the lacing that connects decking to frame. This "fully-laced" Sherpa model provides built-in traction missing from many modern shoes.

Most manufacturers use the terms crampons, cleats, and claws interchangeably, but there are differences. Traditionally, crampons are groups of spikes, while claws are metal bars with serrated edges. Cleats can refer to either style. Crampons provide traction by puncturing the surface and are most useful on ice. If there is loose snow over ice, the crampons' points must be long enough to reach into the ice to be effective. The larger surface area of claws increases resistance and helps on steep snowy slopes. Due to varying conditions, some mountaineering snowshoes have interchangeable or multiple-traction options.

Most modern shoes need at least two traction devices — heel and toe. They are not placed at the heel and toe of the snowshoe, but under the heel and toe of your foot. The toe is the more important one, as it is what you pivot into the slope for traction. The heel device provides stability and additional traction. Some manufacturers put the rear device in different places around the heel to accomplish different purposes, such as to improve traction for traversing slopes.

One traction device that is often overlooked is the lacing that connects the decking to the frame. Many modern snowshoe manufacturers simply wrap the decking around the frame and secure it with rivets, which adds no traction. Others use lacing or clips, which provides additional traction. This is an important fea-

ture, since both the aluminum and decking are slick materials. Sherpa's snowshoes, for example, are "fully laced," with lacing around the entire perimeter of the frame. Tubbs's mountaineering models are "half laced," with lacing only in the rear. Northern Lites uses large clips they call "perimeter cleats" in order to increase traction.

Plastic shoes have offered designers new opportunities for providing traction. Injection molding makes it possible to create any type of pattern on the bottom of the shoe. Therefore, plastic models have tread patterns — just like sneakers — that greatly improve traction. Many are also available with metal spikes for ice.

A similar development is taking place in soft decking materials. Tubbs has recently introduced a patterned synthetic material with additional traction. It would not be a surprise if snowshoe manufacturers borrowed from the design of waxless Nordic skis and added fish-scale patterns to the bottom of deckings in the near future.

Snowshoe traction comes in several forms. Here is a pair of Sherpa fully-laced shoes in action.

SPECIALIZED SNOWSHOES

As snowshoes become more sophisticated, manufacturers are beginning to cater to niche markets. This includes individuals — such as snowboarders, backcountry skiers, and mountaineers — for whom snowshoeing is merely a means of transportation, but not their primary objective. Snowboarders use snowshoes to get them to the top of terrain that is not served by ski lifts. Backcountry skiers have found that snowshoes are more efficient to use than skis, when climbing long ascents. Mountaineers bring along snowshoes when climbing in areas where they may encounter unexpected snow or have to cross snowfields. In addition, they use snowshoes to approach the base of a mountain they intend to summit.

For these markets, snowshoe manufacturers have developed specialized products that include a series of bindings to accommodate footwear used for outdoor activities other than snowshoeing. This allows the snowboarder, skier, or mountaineer to use snowshoes without carrying the weight of extra boots, and to change back and forth quickly and easily.

For backcountry skiers, many manufacturers offer a variety of three-pin bindings, as well as some proprietary bindings, that accommodate Salomon, Rottefella, Voile, and other popular Nordic bindings. Nordic boots are generally well suited for the demands of snowshoeing.

For snowboarders, snowshoe manufacturers offer several different options. Some sell snowshoes with a traditional snowboard binding, consisting of ratcheting straps that encircle the boots. Others offer step-in binding plates to accommodate the newest snowboard technology — boots with locking cleats in the sole. These are different than step-in bindings for mountaineering boots, which consist of toe and heel bails that fit grooves in the boots. Snowboard step-in bindings are similar to clipless pedals on bicycles, with male and female parts on the sole of the boot and the binding, which lock together.

Some snowshoe manufacturers skip the bindings altogether and offer their decks with predrilled thread patterns, which enable snowboarders to mount their choice of snowboard binding plate. All of these systems allow snowboarders to use their snowboarding boots for snowshoeing as well.

For mountaineers who carry snowshoes for occasional use, the development of ultralight and folding models has been key. Anyone who carries a pack in the wilderness quickly learns the importance of saving every extra ounce of weight and using every inch of space wisely. Light snowshoes can be strapped to a backpack without tipping the scales, and folding models can be carried in a fanny pack or side pocket of a backpack.

There are two major folding designs on the market. Snowshoes from Elfman and Sno Trekker can be folded in half. They still take up some room, but fit neatly in a moun-

FIRST AID KIT FOR YOUR SNOWSHOES

Cable ties are the miracle cure for snowshoe ailments. These plastic devices are very light and inexpensive, and can be found at any hardware store in a variety of sizes, so buy and carry an assortment. They are plastic strips with ridges along their length, which pass through a locking slot forming a circle. You can tighten a cable tie as much as you want, but you cannot reloosen it. They can be used to replace broken rivets on decking, by securing the material to the frame. They can also be used to affix splints to snowshoe frames, or fix backpacks, clothing, and other equipment.

In addition to cable ties, consider carrying metal wire or sturdy string, both of which have a wide variety of uses. In a pinch, if you have no other means of affixing something, use the metal wicket from an Alpine ski lift ticket, which someone in your group almost always has hanging on his or her jacket. Duct tape is another "cure-all" used by outdoor folk, but be advised, it doesn't work very well in the cold.

Multi-tools, such as the Leatherman, are the ideal repair device for snowshoes and all other outdoor gear. The Swiss-army knife of tools, these devices usually take the form of folding pliers, with lots

continued on page 46

of other goodies jammed in, including wire cutters, knives, screwdrivers, and even socket sets.

The most common snowshoe problem requiring first aid — especially on wooden shoes — is a broken frame. This can be fixed by splinting. Find two suitable sticks several inches long, and attach one to the top and one to the bottom of the break in the frame with cable ties, string, or tape. Broken aluminum frames can be splinted from within, by jamming a piece of stick the same diameter as the frame into either end of the break.

If you break a buckle or strap on your binding, you can often substitute one from your pack (assuming you're wearing one) or another piece of gear. The accessory straps used to lash loose items to the outside of your pack work well.

Although it's unlikely, you can puncture the decking of a modern snowshoe. Some decking materials will not rip around the puncture and can be left untreated. If you do feel the need to repair the hole, try using a repair kit for tents or one for Gore-Tex clothing, which will include adhesive patches of sturdy material.

taineering pack's shovel pocket and assemble in seconds. Powder Wings manufactures shock-corded aluminum frames that are similar to folding tent poles, and can be totally disassembled. They can be split into parts the size of a water bottle and stashed in small pockets, but take several minutes and some practice to reassemble. Both styles offer fully featured mountaineering models that can be used on backcountry terrain.

Mountaineers often wear hard-shelled, plastic, insulated boots that accommodate crampons and keep their feet warm in extremely cold climates. These boots work well with two piece step-in crampon bindings attached to the snowshoes. Many snowshoe manufacturers, including Ursus, Sherpa, and Tubbs, offer such systems.

FOOTWEAR
AND
OTHER GEAR

Technological improvements have not been confined to snowshoes; footwear designs have improved, as well. Of course, this makes footwear selection more confusing than ever. (See "Footwear Selection Guide," on page 52 for helpful guidelines regarding footwear selections.) Boots have become more specialized, and for the first time manufacturers are actually making models for snow-shoeing. The advantage of this trend is that you can get the perfect shoe to fit your needs, without compromising. The disadvantage is that it makes snowshoeing more complicated and expensive, when it doesn't need to be.

Many first-time snowshoers expect to walk on the snow. Not so! Snowshoes increase your flotation, but you still sink, unless you are walking on a frozen surface. How much you sink depends on local snow conditions — in light-powder areas, like Colorado and Utah, you will sink more than in areas that get wetter snow, such as the Northeast. This goes back to the moisture content of the snow (see Chapter 2). You will also sink farther in fresh snow than "older" snow that has become compacted due to gravity and wind.

Since you do sink, and snow does accumulate on the top of your snow-shoes, the first requirement of

One of the virtues of snowshoeing is that you can make do with whatever you have on hand so long as your feet remain comfortable and dry.

will not breathe as well as a water-resistant one, and sweaty feet that do not breathe can lead to cold toes.

If you are taking relatively short trips, or snowshoeing in dry, light powder, you can get away with a water-resistant boot. If you are going on all-day hikes, or traveling in wetter, heavier snow, it makes sense to go with a truly waterproof model.

footwear is water resistance. As in clothing, there is a trade-off between water resistance and breathability (see Chapter 9). A totally waterproof boot, despite manufacturers' claims, simply

The height of the boots you

■

THE TRUTH ABOUT WATERPROOF

There are four ways to make your footwear waterproof, each of which has pros and cons. Choosing the right one depends on what other uses you have in mind for your boots. Remember that in any design, in any material, the stitches are the weak link, since they make holes in the material. The more stitches, the more likely the boot will leak. Quality footwear has minimal stitching, and tape

covers the inside of the seams.

WATERPROOF MATERIALS

The simplest way to make an item waterproof is to make it out of waterproof material — rubber bars the best. Rubber completely blocks moisture from entering. The disadvantage is that rubber also blocks moisture from exiting, so boots made of rubber do not breathe at all, and will trap sweat, resulting in cold feet. They also lack support and generally don't fit closely enough for sporting activities. Hard-shell moun-

choose will also depend on snow conditions. Since you sink deeper in light, western snow, your boots need to be higher to keep snow from entering the top of the boot (unless you use gaiters). At the other extreme are very packed surfaces, such as the groomed trails many snowshoe races are held on. Since snowshoes do not sink on this surface, and little or no snow accumulates on top of the decking, many racers use ordinary running shoes, which are favored for their comfort and light weight.

ANY OLD THING WILL DO

If you are a novice snowshoer, footwear selection need not be a big concern. Chances are you already have something in your closet that

Once you've got your snowshoes, chances are your closet will provide all the other necessary gear, including footwear. Hiking boots or work boots and a pair of warm wool knee socks suffice.

taineering boots, on the other hand, offer a much better fit. Made of stiff plastic, these are usually waterproof.

WATERPROOF LININGS

Many boots are lined with materials like Gore-Tex or Sympatex, which are waterproof, somewhat-breathable layers of fabric. Boots lined with this material breathe better, and can be made of non-waterproof materials, such as leather, suede, or Cordura. It was the invention of fabrics such as Gore-Tex and Sympatex that made

lightweight hiking boots popular. The disadvantage of waterproof linings is that although your feet stay dry, the outer fabric of the boots still gets wet, which increases weight and compromises breathability.

COATINGS

The traditional method of waterproofing boots was to rub some type of coating over them, such as a silicon-based product, or mink oil. Now there are a variety of

continued on page 50

advanced solutions available for all types of materials. When using them, make sure to apply more than one coat to the boots, and extra to the seams. The advantages of coatings are that they prevent any part of the fabric from becoming wet, and, therefore, allow for the purchase of less-expensive footwear, which can then be treated. The disadvantage is that the coatings wear off and need to be reapplied, which is time and labor intensive. The coatings can also compromise breathability, and, frankly, some just don't work.

LINERS

A recent development is the waterproof sock, made of Gore-Tex or other waterproof fabric. The one disadvantage of wearing waterproof liners is that your footwear still gets soaked. The advantage is that these socks give you great versatility, and can be worn with any footwear, making your cross-country boots, hiking boots, mountain biking shoes, or even tennis sneakers effectively waterproof.

will work. Hiking boots are your best bet, if you own them. You can also use work boots, as long as you wear adequate wool socks for warmth. Many people think that big rubber pac boots, like traditional Sorels, are a natural for snowshoeing. This is not the case. They are heavy, do not fit tightly, and may actually be too warm. Basically, for your first few snowshoe outings, anything that keeps your feet reasonably warm and dry, while providing enough fit and support to keep you comfortable, will be just fine.

Medium- to lightweight hiking boots are the best all-around choice so long as they are at least water-resistant and provide ankle support and protection.

A STEP UP

If you are buying new boots for snowshoeing, the features to look for are water resistance, warmth, fit, and support. The best all-around choice is a quality, lightweight hiking boot. While a traditional, heavier leather boot is preferable for back-

If extending your running/fitness season through the winter months is your ambition, don't look further than your running shoes for footwear. The groomed or packed trails you'll work out on don't require boots, and you'll be grateful for the comfort and light weight.

packing, snowshoeing does not place as much strain on your ankles, so you can get by with the moderate ankle support offered by a day hiker boot. You — and your feet — will appreciate the lighter weight load. In most cases, you should get a boot that comes above the ankle for protection.

As discussed above, whether you select waterproof or water-resistant footwear is a decision you should make based on your usage and snow conditions in your area. Warmth is provided by wearing layers of socks. Your boots should allow room for a liner, a medium-weight pair of wool socks, and an additional pair if necessary (see page 138 for more on socks).

Insulated boots keep your feet warmer, but lack the flexibility needed to be comfortable in milder weather. But non-insulated hiking boots can be used all year long, and adapted to most

Newly-popular low-top approach shoes combined with gaiters are a great option for racers.

If mountaineering is your game, ultra-warm hard-shell boots designed to accept crampons are the answer, but for most snowshoers, even serious ones, they are overkill.

weather conditions by using a layered system of socks. There is, however, a limit to how much insulation you can add to a properly fitting pair of hiking boots through the use of socks. So if you expect to snowshoe regularly in unusually cold conditions, or plan on camping in the bitter cold, then one of the more specialized boots described below is your best choice.

Remember, snowshoeing is an aerobic sport, and you become much warmer while doing it. This goes for your feet as well. When you see boots rated for comfort in very low temperatures — such as -40°F — they are generally for people who are outside but fairly inactive, such as ski-lift attendants or football fans. The body heat that you generate while snowshoeing will go a long way toward keeping your feet warm, and in boots rated for very cold weather, you may actually overheat.

As with most footwear, fit is everything. Remember that snowshoeing is really just another form of walking. On hills and mountains, it is

FOOTWEAR SELECTION GUIDE

① CASUAL SNOWSHOEING — LESS THAN ONE HOUR
Any footwear that is comfortable, and reasonably warm and water resistant.

② CASUAL SNOWSHOEING — MORE THAN ONE HOUR
Hiking boots with liners and wool socks.

③ HALF- OR FULL-DAY HIKES
Lightweight, waterproof hiking boots, liners, one or more layers of wool socks, and gaiters.

④ EXTREME COLD, WINTER CAMPING
Winter utility boots with liners and a variety of socks.

⑤ EXPEDITIONS
Hard-shell mountaineering boots.

⑥ RUNNING/RACING
Approach shoes — high top, or low top with gaiters; on packed surfaces, regular running shoes.

the same as hiking. So buy a boot you would be comfortable walking or hiking in. Workboots, pac boots, and many other types of shoes do not fulfill this requirement. Just as in walking, hiking, or running, ill-fitting footwear will cause blisters when snowshoeing.

Some hiking boots are now being made with indentations in the front and back to accept the bails of crampons; they are standard on mountaineering boots. While generally more expensive, boots that include these indentations give you the flexibility to use not only crampons with your snowshoes, but also step-in bindings, which are easier to take on and off and generally fit and stay on better (see Chapter 2).

High-top lightweight hiking boots are the best all-around choice: they are comfortable, reasonably waterproof and warm; and provide plenty of ankle support.

OTHER OPTIONS

A new and popular form of outdoor recreation footwear has taken the market by storm. Depending on the manufacturer, they are called approach shoes, trail runners, or utility cross trainers. They are basically a cross between a hiking boot and a running shoe, and are available in both low- or high-top styles. Manufactures include both venerable bootmakers, such as One Sport and Merrell, and sneaker "giants," such as Nike and Adidas.

Approach shoes have become popular with some snowshoers, especially racers. They can be worn year-round, weigh even less than light-weight hikers, and are more comfortable than hiking boots. Unfortunately, they are also less durable and less water resistant. For racers, approach shoes work fine, because water resistance is less of an issue on packed surfaces. They are also fine for casual snowshoeing (especially when paired with gaiters, see page 55), as well as other sporting activities. But for an all-purpose snowshoeing boot, stick with hikers.

Hard-shell mountaineering boots are another specialized footwear option. If you have a pair, great; you will not have to buy anything else. If you don't own some, get ready for sticker shock as these boots can cost up to $500. They are meant for tech-

Think twice before wearing your trusty Sorels (right): they are heavy, lack support, and can be too warm. Sport utility boots (bottom), are fully waterproof, weigh less, and fit well, but they may be too warm.

nical mountaineering and ice climbing, and are designed to provide a lot of insulation and accept crampons. Hard-shell mountaineering boots work well with step-in bindings on snowshoes, and are the natural choice if you are tackling a cold, high peak or traversing Antarctica. For most snowshoers, however — even serious ones — they are overkill.

WINTER 4 X 4S

Want to be on the cutting edge? If so, get yourself a pair of winter utility boots. This is a new breed of footwear, created to meet a growing demand from winter campers, snowmobilers, and snowshoers.

In the winter of 1995, the first winter utility boot — the Trukke — was introduced. Trukke's inventor, Rich Breuner, describes them as "winter sports utility footwear [that are] not sport specific." Breuner goes on, "I was trying to address the weakness in the design of the pac

boot . . . warm, heavy boots with no fit characteristics. I wanted something less cumbersome that fits well and has better traction." The result is an odd-looking boot made of neoprene, with a fairly rigid sole, removable fleece liner, and straps and buckles to retain the heel. The boots have acquired something of a cult status; they are especially appreciated by people who spend a long time in the snow, but are active — like snow-making crews at ski resorts.

Following on Trukke's heels are other reputable bootmakers chasing the winter utility market. Sorel, long known for their ultrawarm boots that are loved by ice fishermen and lift attendants alike, has jumped in with their Trailhead series — three different boots developed for snowshoers and cold-weather enthusiasts. Technica, well known for both hiking and ski boots, is also launching a winter sport line. More bootmakers are sure to follow this lead in the near future.

What all of these boots have in common is that they are waterproof, provide warmth, and fit well. Manufacturers have developed them for those who are out in the snow and cold for prolonged periods, and need athletic comfort and support. The only drawback to these boots is that they may just be too warm. An active day of snowshoeing generates a lot of heat, and these boots are insulated for fairly extreme temperatures. If you find yourself comfortable in hiking boots and wool socks, there is no need to buy a pair of winter utility boots. But if you have a problem with cold toes, these may very well be your salvation.

A pair of quality gaiters keeps snow out of your boots, important to snowshoers, who kick up far more snow than cross-country skiers do.

FOOTWEAR ACCESSORIES
Gaiters

Gaiters are not required for snowshoeing, but I highly recommend them. These water-resistant fabric sleeves, which wrap around the tops of your boots and cover your lower legs, serve several purposes. Most importantly, they keep snow out of your boots. When snowshoeing briskly, even in heavy snow, the white stuff has a tendency to fly everywhere, and land inside your boots. Gaiters prevent this from happening.

Gaiters also protect your boots from moisture, as many cover up the laces and most of the exterior. Quality gaiters attach to a ring near the toe of your boot, or hook onto your lowest lace, and have a string or strap that

passes under the instep of your boot, drawing the gaiter low and snug. This leaves only your toe exposed.

Once you get the hang of snowshoeing, and realize that falls are uncommon, you may decide to wear tights, fleece pants, or the newer stretch fleece tights, all of which are great for snowshoeing, but aren't waterproof. Gaiters come to the rescue by protecting the lower part of your pant legs from spraying snow.

Finally, gaiters add versatility to your footwear choices. They allow you to wear lower boots in deeper, dryer snow, and low approach shoes for snowshoe running or racing, thus decreasing your weight load and increasing your comfort. In addition,

Cross-country poles are fine, but tele-scoping trekking poles like these can be adjusted to suit snowshoers of different heights, have interchangeable tips, col-lapse for storage or carrying on a pack, and can also serve as avalanche probes.

you can use one pair of boots in many different types of snow when you add a good pair of gaiters.

Gaiters come in a wide variety of heights: some cover just the area between boot and pant cuff; others come up to your knee. Even with quality water-proof hiking boots of a decent height, chances are you will get some snow in your boots. Save yourself the trouble and the dis-comfort — buy some gaiters. Full-height gaiters run from $35 to $40 (EMS, REI) to $70 to $100 (Outdoor Research).

Booties and Toe Covers

Some snowshoes feature insu-lated bindings, neoprene sleeves that you put around your boots before tightening the laces or straps. You can increase insu-lation on your own, without buying insulated bindings, by using neoprene booties or toe covers.

Neoprene is a closed-cell mate-rial used in the construction of recre-ational clothing and gear — from SCUBA wet suits to winter gloves. It stretches to fit snugly, and traps a lot of air, which provides insulation in a thin layer.

Neoprene booties or toe covers go on the outside of your boots. They provide additional warmth, and will add some water protection to your boots, as well. If you enjoy using lightweight hiking boots and find conditions a bit colder than you're used to, try adding a pair.

OTHER GEAR
Poles

After buying snowshoes and boots, you will probably want to look at purchasing a pair of poles. Many consider them to be optional equipment, and in some cases, this can be true. If you are purely a casual, recreational snowshoer, strolling on relatively flat terrain, then you can cer-tainly get by without poles. But poles make snowshoeing easier and safer, give you a better workout, and are very beneficial to use during long excursions or on extreme terrain (see "Using Your Poles," page 77).

Many snowshoers make do with ski poles that they already own. If you have cross-country poles, and use them for snow-shoeing, you sacrifice little in the way of performance. Downhill poles are more of a trade-off, since they are too short. They will work, and I have used them without incident. However, they are not the best choice, and some — such as the newer downhill poles that have tiny baskets that go into the snow under pressure — are not at all adequate for snowshoeing.

If you do not own any poles and are buying them for the first time, you may want to consider cross-country poles, as they are less expensive than mountaineering poles. If price is no object, hiking, trekking, or mountaineering poles, as they are variously called, are the cream of the crop.

Using poles makes sense. They're an aid in climbing and descending steeps and help shift some of the workout from your legs to your upper body.

These poles tend to be stronger, and, therefore, more durable than ski poles. They often have interchangeable tips, so you can use sharp points for ice, and switch to blunter tips for hiking in the summer. Some even have threaded tripod mounts so you can use them as monopods for photographic purposes.

The real benefit of mountaineering poles is that they telescope, and can be adjusted to various lengths. This enables them to be used by several individuals of different heights. When not in use, they collapse and store easily in or on a pack.

poles by making the uphill one shorter and/or the downhill one longer, so that you can have contact with the ground on both sides while keeping your shoulders level.

Before buying a set of poles, make sure you "try them on for size." For correct length, your elbow should be bent to slightly less than a right angle when holding the pole in front of you, with your hand slightly higher than your elbow. Err on the side of poles that are

An expedition up Mount Rainier, Washington State. Ski poles provide an extra measure of balance and endurance when carrying a heavy pack.

Telescoping poles are also valuable during long traverses. Snowshoes are not really designed for traversing slopes (see Chapter 4), but occasionally you may find yourself with no choice. In this case, you can take advantage of your telescoping

too long rather than too short. Bear in mind that the few inches of pole beneath the basket will be under the snow; so if you are trying out poles in the store, invert them and grasp below the basket to simulate losing the pointy tip.

No matter what type of poles you choose, I am sure you will soon realize that they are an important snowshoe accessory. Poles can help you maintain your balance, making snowshoeing easier and inspiring confidence. They can also assist you in getting up if you fall, and are very useful when climbing or descending steep hills, or when turning around. Finally, using poles allows you to shift some of the physical load from your legs to your arms, which not only gives you a full-body workout, but also prolongs the amount of time you can snowshoe before your legs become fatigued. This transfer of workload can be surprisingly beneficial to your leg muscles after a long day on the trail.

Ice Axes

Another balance aid is the long-handled ice ax. If you are an ice climber who combines snowshoeing with scaling frozen waterfalls, you will already own and know how to use an ice ax. By affixing a basket to the end of the handle (most ice axes can accommodate this), you have a pole. Voila!

For the rest of us, an ice ax is a foreign device. The reason why a snowshoer would carry one rather

If you snowshoe where sliding down ice- or snow-covered steeps is a danger, an ice ax and the skill to use it in self arrest can be a lifesaver.

than a regular pole is the same reason why expedition mountaineers use them: to stop themselves when sliding on ice or snow. This technique is called a self arrest (see page 109). If you do not snowshoe where this danger is a possibility, you will not need an ice ax. If you do, you should take self-arrest lessons from a mountaineering school. Self arrest is not difficult to learn, but without the skill to safely stop your slide, the ax is worse than useless, it's a danger to you.

Daypacks

Some type of pack is a necessity for any snowshoer who is going farther than a few hundred yards on a golf course. You need somewhere to stash those extra layering essentials, like a fleece vest, hat, and gloves. You also will be carrying food and water, a compass and map, matches, a first aid kit, maybe a camera and binoculars, and whatever else strikes your fancy. You would have trouble fitting all this into your pockets.

There are several choices in daypacks, depending on your load. The longer the trip, or the more uncertain the weather conditions, the more you will have to carry.

For short excursions, fanny

mesh outer pockets for additional storage, special camera and key pockets, and compression straps for cinching down an oversized load or attaching a jacket. A few are even modular systems,

A fanny pack (left) should follow you everywhere, even on a half-day outing. Day packs (right) should feature waist belts and plenty of pockets.

packs work well because there are no straps across your shoulders and they are very comfortable. Fanny packs have been vastly improved from the original single-pocket designs. Many of the better-quality models have substantial storage, and some even hold external water bottles — a handy feature, as long as your water does not freeze.

When purchasing a fanny pack, choose one with a padded back for protection from objects inside the pack rubbing against you, and either an anatomically molded design that fits comfortably against the small of your back or a suspension model. These are designed to increase air flow, utilizing a mesh backing that lies against your body, and an air-space between the mesh and the pack. This feature is more important in the summer, when sweat coming through your outer layer is an issue.

Better-quality fanny packs have that allow the size of the pack to be changed depending on your storage requirements. However, there are limits to what you can carry. Before you go out and buy a fanny pack, think about whether you are also going to need an overnight pack. Many overnight packs now have detachable top pockets that convert into fanny packs, giving you two packs for the price of one.

Another time-tested daypack design is the rucksack, which is usually one big compartment; some with smaller pockets or added features. These packs ride high on your back, are comfortable, and hold more than a fanny pack. Make sure you try moving around with it on in the store; if the pack flops or rides up and down, don't buy it — you won't be comfortable carrying it on the trail. Make sure the pack you buy has a waist belt, which keeps the pack from shifting.

The largest-capacity daypacks are scaled-down versions of overnight internal-frame backpacks. While these internal-suspension daypacks are considerably more expensive, they are worth it, if you plan to carry substantial loads. These packs have a slim profile, which minimizes the effect on your balance, and usually are equipped with useful extras, such as straps to hold poles, ice ax loops, and compression straps for compacting loads.

Many pack manufacturers, such as North Face and Osprey, are now making packs specifically intended to carry snowboards. Most of these designs also work well for snowshoes, so it becomes a simple matter of stepping out of the snowshoes and onto the snowboard at the top of a run, than 'boarding down with the snowshoes in your pack.

Overnight Packs

An overnight pack is one that is carried on trips that last longer than a day. The most important factor to consider when buying an overnight pack is the length of your trip, since

HYDRATION PACKS

Since the introduction of the Camelbak, back-mounted hydration systems have taken the outdoor recreation market by storm. These are flexible plastic bladders that hold liquid, usually 64 to 90 ounces. The bladder is housed in a small, trim pack with shoulder straps and a waist belt. A plastic drinking tube from the bladder extends over your shoulder and attaches to your collar or shoulder strap. To drink, all you have to do is turn your head and bite the valve.

Hand-free access to large volumes of fluid is convenient, and ensures more regular drinking than the occasional water bottle break.

For this reason, these packs have become very popular with bikers and other sport enthusiasts. Even rock-and-roll stars use them during concerts. Manufacturers have expanded the line, and now offer the bladders in conjunction with a variety of daypacks, and companies such as Osprey, Vortex and Gregory are incorporating them into overnight packs.

The drawback in winter is that the water tends to freeze, when carried on your back. The only practical solution is to wear both the bladder and the hose under your clothing. A small streamlined model that is comfortable beneath a shell is best to carry when snowshoeing and cross-country skiing.

that will determine how much storage capacity you will need.

When making a decision regarding pack size, ask yourself how long you seriously intend to winter camp. Winter camping is much more arduous than fair-weather camping. I rarely spend more than two nights out on a trip in winter, whereas in summer I might go for a week. Unless you are engaging in hut-to-hut tours or backcountry mountaineering adventures, beware the tendency to overestimate the length of your winter camping trips.

In addition, since you will carry a lot more gear in winter, and everything is bigger — from your tent to your sleeping bag — a pack that claims to be good for "a week of lightweight camping" might only be good for one or two winter nights. For winter camping, I find that you can expect no more

than two thirds of the capacity that a pack is rated for, so a pack designed for a week-long summer backpacking trip is an appropriate size for four winter nights.

In many ways, shopping for a snow-shoeing pack is easier than for a backpacking model, because the field is narrower. Since it is important to minimize the effect of the pack on your balance and center of gravity, and maintain unencumbered use of your arms and a full range of motion, the use of an external-frame pack for snowshoeing is not practical. Internal-frame packs are best, because they offer a streamlined, body-hugging design.

The suspension unit, or the frame itself, is the most important element of an internal-frame pack, and will make the difference between you being comfortable or miserable. Most high-end pack companies try to differentiate themselves on the basis of fit and suspension, so it is important to try on models from several manufacturers.

Before buying,

put a hefty load into the pack and try it out on a walk. If it does not fit comfortably in the store, it certainly will not in the mountains.

Pack fitting has become more precise in recent years, and most packs now come in different sizes. Some are sized for men and women. In addition, many companies offer a variety of sizes in hip-belts and shoulder straps. Fitting a back-pack has become an art form akin to tailoring, so it is important to purchase your pack from a qualified outfitter.

A snowshoer sets off on a day's outing with gaiters to keep his feet warm, poles for balance, and a day pack stocked with food, water, and spare clothes.

There are numerous specialized features available on today's packs; some are useful, some are useless. While there are no packs designed specifically for snowshoers, there are packs marketed for skiers, climbers, and snowboarders that have features that are beneficial to snowshoers. The most important ones are:

WAND POCKETS These are small vertical pockets on the sides of the pack, designed to keep the tips of tent poles in place, with straps farther up for securing the poles. These are also very useful for carrying snowshoeing poles, especially telescoping ones, without using up internal space.

SLEEPING BAG COMPARTMENT While somewhat of a luxury, this feature is great for winter camping, since it is important to keep your bag dry. A separate zippered sleeping bag compartment on the bottom of the pack allows for easy access and protects your bag from wet clothes or spilled food. Some packs even include a built-in stuffsack for easy loading.

SHOVEL POCKET An external shovel pocket is good for carrying a shovel, but is also a good place in which to secure your snowshoes during approach hikes.

SNOWBOARD CARRIER Some packs now have optional harnesses for attaching a snowboard to the back, and these work very well for carrying your snowshoes.

EXPANDABILITY Packs are becoming increasingly modular, and some offer optional attachments such as day-packs and extra pockets that clip on. This allows you to purchase a slightly smaller pack and still use it for longer trips.

DETACHABLE PARTS Many overnight packs include detachable top pockets that become fanny packs or daypacks — great for making brief excursions from your campsite, or for using by themselves on daytrips.

ICE-AX LOOPS AND DAISY CHAINS If you carry an ice ax, you will appreciate these loops. In addition, a daisy chain, which is a series of webbing loops, makes it easy to attach a variety of extra items to the outside of the pack, increasing the storage capacity.

There are many other options available on overnight packs; you will have to decide for yourself whether or not they are worth the extra money. Buy a pack that fits well, and includes all of the features you will need: this is one piece of gear you don't want to skimp on — it will come back to haunt you out on the trail.

WALKING ON SNOW

So you've borrowed or rented equipment, put your snowshoes on, and tightened up your bindings. You're ready.

Now what?

It's time to walk.

Start by putting one foot in front of the other. It's that simple. If you are using poles, plant the pole opposite the foot that you are moving forward, just as you would naturally swing your right arm forward when you stride with your left foot. For instance, if you are about to step forward with your right foot, firmly plant your left pole well out in front of you. Then switch. Now you are moving.

I recommend a golf course for your first outing, as it is wide open, with some gentle grades and a few steep hills. This is perfect terrain on which to first try the sport. You can remain in the area where you parked your car, and head back if you start to get cold.

Once you get the hang of walking in snowshoes, take the time to notice how the particular design of the snowshoes you have borrowed or rented affects your actual performance. If the shoes you are using are a newer model, they are probably small enough so that you can take a natural stride without worrying about the inside edges of the shoes hitting each other. This is especially true of

Bryce Canyon National Park, Utah. Snowshoeing is nearly as easy as walking. Once you learn the length and width of your snowshoeing stride, you're ready to explore.

(modern) shoes first, and give them a try.

In addition to the side-to-side clearance issue, you also need to consider the longer front-to-back size of snowshoes when walking. Beginners often step on the back of the lead shoe when taking a step, and can stumble. To avoid this, you may have to take slightly longer-than-normal strides, especially if your weight requires you to use larger shoes.

While most modern shoes do not have a tail, or have a very short one, some wooden models may have tails that are nearly a foot long. If this is the case with your shoes, make sure you are careful not to cross or step on the tails during your stride.

Learning the length and width of your stride will come quickly to you, and by the end of your first few dozen steps you will be ready for more advanced techniques.

TURNING AROUND

Snowshoes have no reverse gear. While it is not impossible to back up, it is not recommended, as the shoes will not cooperate. Snowshoe bindings are designed to pivot, which provides a lot of advantages, such as enabling you to raise the toe for the next step, helping you to climb hills, and allowing you to shake loose snow off of the decking. In reverse however, this pivot is a hindrance. The tail of the shoe goes down as soon as

the asymmetrical models. If you are using bigger shoes or older symmetrical models, however, you will have to exaggerate your stride, swinging your foot out to the side in a slightly circular path with each step to avoid hitting the side of the other shoe. This motion, while slight, requires a lot of extra effort and will quickly tire you. It also uses hip muscles that are probably not used to this motion, and may, therefore, leave you quite sore afterward. In Quebec this condition is known as mal de raquette — the pain of the snowshoe. If you have borrowed a wider or a symmetrical pair of shoes, and have experienced this, don't get frustrated and give up on the sport — rent a pair of smaller

you raise your foot off the ground, and digs in as you try to step backward. In order to succeed, you have to lift each foot quite high and go slowly and carefully — a dangerous and nearly impossible feat on a steep slope. Therefore, it's much better to learn the right way to reverse direction.

If you have room, the easiest way to turn around is to walk in a semicircle, going forward the whole time. But for tight spaces or on slopes, you will need to learn how to use the "kick turn." If you enjoy skiing, you may already be familiar with this technique, which is considerably easier to execute with snowshoes, since they are much shorter than skis.

The kick turn is a fairly simple maneuver: Plant your poles firmly at your sides for balance. Lift one foot, turn it 180 degrees, and place it down. Make sure this foot is planted firmly, then shift your weight onto it. Now your feet are facing in opposite directions. Pick up your second foot and swing it all the way around so it ends up parallel to your first foot. That's all there is to it. Now you're going the other way.

THE SCIENCE OF TAKING A BREAK

In any sport that requires exertion for extended periods of time, you have to learn to pace yourself. When snowshoeing, there are some special pacing techniques that you can learn to make a long trip fun rather than exhausting.

The rest step is a simple, yet difficult-to-grasp trick that can mean the difference between snowshoeing for an hour and snowshoeing all day. This step may be familiar to seasoned

The kick turn is simple. Plant your poles at your sides for balance. 1) Lift one foot, turn it 180 degrees, place it down, and shift your weight to it. 2) Pick up your second foot and swing it around. 3) You've reversed directions.

CONDITIONING

Part of your fun and safety on snowshoes will depend on what kind of shape you're in. If you rarely exercise, or stick to walking, you will probably not want to head out on an all-day ascent of a 5000-foot peak. On the other hand, if you run, bike, and ski regularly, and are fit, you will be more able to jump into snowshoeing aggressively.

Snowshoeing is a highly aerobic activity, and deciding how much to do requires you to be honest with yourself. Even on flat ground at a moderate pace, snowshoeing takes more energy than walking, due to the added weight, resistance, and use of different muscles. If your normal fitness routine consists of a two-mile walk, you are best off starting with a stroll on a golf course and seeing how long it takes before you are tired and ready to stop for the day.

Snowshoeing in hilly terrain at a brisker pace requires much more energy. Many participants, myself included, feel it requires more exertion than cross-country skiing over the same terrain. A strenuous one-hour hike on snowshoes can be more taxing than running the equivalent distance, so do not set out on such a trip unless you are confident in your fitness abilities. Likewise, a summit hike, even on a small peak, is far more strenuous than summer hiking.

Like any other sport, the best way to prepare for more difficult snowshoeing trips is to build up to them by doing shorter distances. Start with a short hike that you know you can do on fairly level ground, maybe an hour long. Then, every time you go out, add a little more. Not only will this build up your endurance, but it will train your muscles for the sport. Repetitive motions inspire "muscle memory," and as your muscles become accustomed to a new motion, it becomes easier.

There is nothing wrong with getting tired or feeling exhausted at the end of a day's activity. In fact, this proves that you accomplished something and can be rewarding in and of itself. But there is a big difference between returning home exhausted, and being exhausted several miles into the woods. The latter is potentially dangerous, and even if it ends without incident, can lead to a lack of desire to ever snowshoe again.

For your first outing, choose a wide open spot with only gentle grades up or down. In a matter of minutes you'll adjust your stride to accommodate the snowshoes. Ski poles aid balance.

hikers and backpackers, but many hikers who could benefit from its use don't know how and when to do so.

The secret lies in taking a brief rest right in the middle of each step, much the way your heart takes a split-second rest between beats. This is achieved by transferring the weight of your body from your leg muscles to your skeleton for a moment at the conclusion of each step. Here's the basic process:

Put your right foot forward, and after transferring all your weight onto it, lock your right knee and pause for a moment before continuing. Then, with your right leg still locked, bring your left foot forward, plant it, transfer all your weight onto it, and then lock your left knee. Pause for a

second and continue. The rests are very brief, so that you are not stopping after every step, just "pausing."

While these tiny pauses may not feel like much, over time they accomplish a lot. When you lock your knee, the long lower and upper bones of the leg become one rigid unit, and bear all your weight with no need for muscular assistance. You are now carrying your weight on three "poles": the two in your hand and your leg. These brief rests for your leg muscles are far more effective at increasing endurance than occasional longer breaks.

If the whole concept of the rest step seems odd to you, as it probably will, try it on dry ground. Trying it out on snow is not necessary. However, for the most effective demonstration, practice the rest step while going uphill, since this is when you will most likely use it on the trail. In a short time, you will notice the pronounced difference that using the rest step makes.

In deep snow, especially the lighter powder most common in the West, there is another brief pause that can increase your endurance. When you plant your forward foot, pause for a moment before transferring all of your weight. This is sometimes called stamping, and although some people confuse it with the rest step, it's purpose is quite different. The objective is to firm up the snow so it better supports your weight.

Snow is fickle, and becomes denser with time and under other conditions (see Chapter 2). One of these is pressure. If you first compact the snow under your foot slightly with pressure, when you transfer your full weight onto it, you will not sink as far. The less you sink, the less work you have to do to raise your foot back out of the snow for the next step. This is the principle behind stamping.

To get the feel for stamping, try an easy experiment. Put one foot

CROSS-TRAINING

Snowshoeing can be a great part of your fitness routine. It is highly aerobic, builds up leg strength, and to a lesser extent, works out your  upper body. To cross-train for snowshoeing, participate in other sports that are similar in terms of muscles used and benefits gained. Running and biking, which utilize the larger muscles of the leg and increase aerobic capacity, are good choices. Cross-country skiing includes an upper-body workout and closely approximates snow-

ahead of the other and apply enough weight to just break the surface of the snow, sinking maybe an inch. Pause and hold your foot there for a couple of seconds. Now transfer your full weight to that foot and see how far it sinks. Bring up your back foot and immediately transfer your full weight onto it as you plant it in the snow. You will sink farther than with your first step. Of course, you should not pause for several seconds on every step, but just for a moment. The longer you pause, however, the greater the compacting effect, and the more you will notice the snow firming up.

BREAKING TRAIL

The same idea of firming up the snow applies to breaking trail: snowshoeing through unbroken snow and laying down fresh tracks. Breaking trail can be tiring, so it is best for groups of snowshoers, like cross-country skiers, to go in single file, taking care to step in the footprints of the person ahead of them.

Some experts estimate that breaking trail requires about 50 percent more energy than following behind. In deep, soft snow, it can feel like even more. For this and other safety reasons, don't snowshoe alone

---

shoeing. Any or all of these activities will enhance your ability to snowshoe and vice versa.

If you are an avid hiker or backpacker, you will be very comfortable snowshoeing. The high leg lifts required on steep ascents, and the weight of a pack will be familiar to you. Indeed, a winter of snowshoeing in the mountains will leave you in better shape than ever for a summer of hiking those same peaks. To practice for snowshoeing, you can wear heavy boots or even ankle weights, and use trekking poles when hiking.

Stair climbers or steppers are also good to use when training for snowshoeing. These devices emphasize high knee lifts and use

of the calf muscles, while building aerobic capacity. The best machines for snowshoe training are the ones that also allow you to exercise your arms.

Weight training can also complement your snowshoeing. Since snowshoeing disproportionately works your quadriceps, it is a good idea to use weight training to strengthen your hamstrings. In addition, strengthening your abdominal muscles will make it easier to lift your shoes high on ascents, and prevent a sore back. And a stronger upper body will allow you to use your poles to relieve more of the load on your legs, thus enabling you to go farther.

A "naturally" groomed trail. Among snowshoers there's no need for grooming machines or snowmobiles. The snowshoe is the ideal trail breaker.

that long. With more people, switch more frequently — as often as every 3 minutes, with the leader going to the back of the line. In a group of several snowshoers, you might get 20 to 30 minutes of rest between your turns at breaking trail. The more the merrier, as each additional snowshoer increases the efficiency of the group. The snow is compacted with every step, so the last person in line has it even easier than those ahead of him.

unless you are very familiar with the sport and the terrain. Since breaking trail requires so much energy, the task should be frequently rotated. When snowshoeing with only one companion, I usually switch positions every 10 to 15 minutes, but in deep powder it is impossible to even go

Switching leaders is also a great equalizer. In hiking, groups often get divided by pace, with one or two speed demons streaking out in front. If you aren't a speed demon, then you're familiar with the following scenario: You are exhausted, hiking as fast as you can to catch up to your companions in front. You come around a turn and find them waiting for you, catching their breath. They are already tired of standing there, so the minute you arrive, they're off again. The slowest person in the group is the one who never gets to rest. This happens in hiking, biking, cross-country skiing, and other sports. Because of the demands of trailbreaking, however, it does not generally happen in snowshoeing.

THE UPS AND DOWNS OF SNOWSHOEING

Once you have mastered your stride, rest step, stamping, and trailbreaking skills, you are ready for the hills. Mountains and snowshoes are a natural match, because the best snow is usually found in the mountains. Climbing is the most difficult part of snowshoeing, and going down is the most fun.

Climbing the Fall Line

The fall line is the path that a freely rolling object, such as a ball or tire, would take coming down a slope. As a rule of thumb, snowshoers should seek out the fall line and follow it up the mountain whenever possible. It is usually the shortest, most direct, and in many cases (despite the angle), the easiest route up a slope. Exceptions to this rule would be when the grade is simply too steep to navigate, there is danger of an avalanche, or the path is too icy.

Breaking trail in deep, soft powder snow can be tiring. It takes some 50 percent more energy than following behind. To save energy use a technique called stamping (see page 70).

Snowshoes are designed for going forward. The pivot of the binding drives the toe into the ground, which provides traction from front to back. Other traction aids on the shoe, such as the lacing around the frame, work front to back as well. New or old, snowshoes have maximal traction when going forward, since the entire shoe is in contact with the slope. Snowshoes are not designed for traversing slopes, and are not meant to be used on their edges.

Some newer technical models intended for serious mountaineering have repositioned the heel cleats, to provide added stability for when tra-

On firm terrain, the traction provided by your toes and cleats will be perfectly adequate to support you, even on a steep slope. The difficulty comes when there are a few inches of soft, fresh snow over a packed

Regularly switching leaders is the way to share the extra work of breaking trail. It also allows slower walkers to keep pace with faster ones.

versing a slope is necessary. However, even these models are not very stable when used in this fashion. If cutting across a slope can be avoided, by all means avoid it!

base. In this situation, your toes have little to grasp, and your snowshoes tend to slide backward.

For moderate grades that are covered in loose snow, an easy solu-

BE AN EFFICIENCY EXPERT

The rest step, stamping, and other techniques may sound like a lot of complicated and unnecessary additions to a relatively simple sport. But snowshoeing is basically about a transfer of energy from your muscles to the snow. Everything that can be done to make this transfer more efficient reduces your energy output, and, therefore, increases your endurance. For most people, increased endurance translates

into more enjoyment, so it pays to become an efficiency expert.

By hurrying and walking abreast, rather than in single file, even trained athletes can quickly be reduced to a state of exhaustion. Being tired is bad enough, but in the winter, exhaustion can lead to injuries or even hypothermia. But, by taking turns breaking trail, particularly the rest step and stamping, and using your poles correctly, you — and your companions — can enjoy a nice, long, safe trip on snowshoes.

tion to this problem is the herringbone step, similar to the technique used in cross-country skiing. With this step, you turn your toes out so the shoes land at a 45-degree angle, forming a "V." This places a larger surface area in contact with the slope, which limits the amount you will slide backward. If this method still doesn't

When going uphill on dry powder, it's often necessary to take longer strides than usual.

provide enough traction to ascend, you can side step, turning your body perpendicular to the slope and taking small sideward steps up. By doing so, you keep the full length of the shoe against the slope, which provides maximum contact with the snow, and increases resistance. This is a very slow way to go and should only

be used when absolutely necessary. No matter what step you use, it is always best to climb along the fall line, wherever possible.

The herringbone step: turn your toes out so they land at a 45-degree angle to each other, forming a V and limiting backward slide.

the integrity of the snow.

When climbing steep slopes on packed snow, the opposite is true. In this case, you will want to take shorter steps, in order to increase your stability and minimize the amount of time that you are supporting your weight on only one shoe.

When climbing steep slopes on packed snow, take shorter steps and aggressively dig your toe cleats into the surface for stability and traction.

GOING DOWN

Descending slopes on snowshoes can be either fun or scary. The best way to proceed is to survey the terrain ahead. A wide-open slope poses fewer obstacles than a tightly wooded trail. Snow conditions and steepness will dictate your method of descent.

When going uphill on dry powder, it is often necessary to take longer strides than usual. When you break the surface of the snow and firm up your footprint, you also create an unstable area around the footprint. If you step near the footprint hole, the snow around your last step will collapse and slide into the void. Therefore, when the snow is soft and unstable, your footsteps need to be farther apart in order to preserve

If you are faced with a steep, narrow descent, or are at all apprehensive, you can try side stepping, just as you might on a climb. Make sure to plant your poles securely, and get each step firmly set in the snow before taking another.

You can also descend by walking down in a straight line. Again, it is important that you remember to plant your poles firmly before taking each step. Make sure your feet are also

To run slide down wide open hills, take big steps and lift your toes.

well planted, which may mean transferring some weight to your heels. Ideally, you want the shoes to be level with the horizon, not parallel to the slope, since the latter will increase their tendency to slide.

USING YOUR POLES

There are different schools of thought in regard to the best use of poles in snowshoeing. Some experts suggest using your poles to push off behind you and assist in forward motion — as in cross-country skiing. After much trial and error, I have sided with the "forward pole-planting school." Planting the pole in front of you allows you to transfer a lot of your weight to the pole, thus increasing your stability and reducing fatigue. This method also gives you the added bonus of an upper-body workout, greatly increasing the cardiovascular benefits of the sport.

Nowhere are poles more helpful than on steep hills. When climbing, plant your poles firmly to help you maintain your balance while you lift one foot off the ground. With two poles and one leg firmly planted on the ground, you become in essence, a tripod. And as photographers well know, a tripod is very stable. When descending, plant your poles well in front, so that when your foot is placed between them, you do not slide down the mountain.

ally the worst for glissading, since they have better traction and greater resistance.

Another way to glide down a mountain is to take big steps, lifting your toes and sliding a long way with each step. A snowshoeing friend of mine described this as "walking down a sand dune." You go farther with each step, as the snow gives out under your foot. This is sometimes called step sliding. If conditions permit it to be done

Just plain leaping and sliding down a hill on snowshoes can be loads of fun.

Sliding, or glissading, down a mountain is the most fun. There are a few different ways to accomplish this, but all require shifting your weight to your heels, which lifts your toes out of the snow and takes the drag off the cleats. You can then "surf" on your heels. Unfortunately, the snowshoes that are best for climbing are gener-

safely (there are no trees or other obstacles), you can increase the distance traveled with each step by increasing your velocity and run sliding down the slope.

A third method of glissading is to bend at the knees, get your weight way back, and just slide down on your heels. An even more extreme version is to actually sit back on the snow, with the heels of the shoes in front of you and the toes pointing way up. Make sure you snowshoe in waterproof pants if this becomes your preferred method of descent.

My favorite way to slide is to assume a position similar to that of a Telemark skier, with one foot far in front of the other and both knees bent. The front knee is kept at a 90-degree angle, while the back foot is extended well behind the body. This partial crouch and wide stance provide stability, and the back foot functions as a rudder. At the end of each

Assume a Telemark position when glissading in forested areas.

MAN'S (AND WOMAN'S) BEST FRIEND

A dog is truly a wonderful outdoor companion and winter weather is no reason to let your canine friend turn into a couch potato. If your dog likes to run and hike in the summer, he will feel equally at home out in the snow.

One of the best qualities of dogs is that they are always willing. When fresh snow falls and the sun comes out, you may not be able to round up a group of human companions to head out into the great outdoors, but your dog will be ready. Just make sure you reward this loyalty by taking care of your dog's safety and welfare

during your outdoor adventures together.

Veterinarian Ginny Prince knows quite a bit about dogs and the great outdoors. An experienced vet, Ginny is also a stellar athlete, a former national mountain biking champion, and an avid snowshoer, and Telemark and cross-country skier. When the snow stops her from winning mountain bike races, she teaches skiing, or takes to the woods with her dog, George.

"Healthy dogs should be able to easily maintain the pace of a dayhiker. Make sure they do not get too cold, by keeping an eye on

continued on page 80

MAN'S (AND WOMAN'S)
BEST FRIEND
continued from page 79

them for shivering. This mainly happens when they stop, and short-haired dogs are more susceptible.

"Frostbite usually isn't a concern, as dogs have excellent circulation. The biggest problem is their feet, which get irritated and cut from the abrasiveness of the snow. Ice balls form between their toes, and this causes irritation. Usually the dogs can just chew them out, but it is more of a problem in wet, clumpy snow. Even in the Iditarod, the main problem is sore feet, not frostbite. Booties can prevent this, but they often do not fit well, and even if they do, they adversely affect your dog's traction.

"They say that eating snow does not provide enough hydration for dogs, but on day trips I think it does. If you are unsure, you can give the dog supplemental water.

"One other concern is fatigue. In deep snow, which you usually have if you're wearing snowshoes, the dog's feet break through and sink, just as yours would. This is much more tiring, and the dog might get fatigued, even if he or she could normally go 20 times farther than you. The problem here is that even if you stop and turn around, the dog might be unwilling to continue, and if he's too big to carry, you're in trouble. Be alert if your dog begins to tire, and don't go too far from your starting point."

big step slide, you switch the position of the front and back feet. I particularly like this technique in forested areas, as it seems to offer better steering and more control.

T E C H N I Q U E S
F O R
S T E E P S

If you enjoy snowshoeing, sooner or later you will want to try climbing a big mountain. Although the same dayhikes that you enjoyed in the summer become much more difficult when mired by deep, unbroken snow and slick steep patches, they are far from impossible. In fact, just about any trail that can be hiked can be ascended with snowshoes.

Get used to your snowshoes and practice the basic techniques before setting out to conquer the big peaks. If you are planning an aggressive climb, make sure to leave yourself enough time. A two-hour summer hike can take five hours or longer when there is a lot of snow. Also

make sure that you dress accordingly and carry safety gear (see Chapters 8 and 9). There are several factors — like the cold and shorter days — that need to be considered when snowshoeing in the mountains. A relatively benign injury or mishap can turn tragic in the winter, so be prepared, and never take the same risks that you would in the summer.

Many slopes are too steep to walk up with just your toes for traction, and too long to attempt using the herringbone or side step. There are, however, several additional techniques that you can use to make your way up seemingly impossible grades.

Any trail that can be hiked in summer can be ascended with snowshoes in winter, and some steeps are easier to tackle with snowshoes. This climber is using his poles for balance and to bring upper body strength to his effort. He is taking long strides through moderately deep powder.

THE TOE KICK

The most useful of all climbing techniques is the toe kick. It is beautiful in its simplicity, yet many new snowshoers rarely think to try it. The technique is widely used by winter mountaineers wearing regular boots, and works even better with snowshoes on.

Instead of placing your snowshoe on the slope and digging your boot toe in, kick the toe of the snowshoe itself into the slope. This is harder to do the more upturned your snowshoe toe is. A good swift kick should bury the snowshoe up to your foot. You will now be standing on a step made of snow, and can lift the other shoe and do likewise. When you are done, the pattern left behind in the snow will resemble a staircase.

This is the one time in snowshoeing when it is better to lead than to follow. The trail is very stable for the trailbreaker, but as others follow, the steps often collapse, leaving just two long furrows in the snow. This is particularly common in dry powder.

On many steep climbs, the traction of your cleats along with digging the toe of your boot into the snow is all you need.

Kicking the toe of your boot into the snow (left) makes many climbs easier, but for really steep grades you should use the toe kick, digging the toe of the snowshoe itself into the snow.

If there is adequate room, it may be better to go two abreast rather than single file. Once the steps are broken out completely, it is difficult to get any traction.

Adequate snow depth is necessary to toe kick. In the East there is often far less snow on the high steeps where wind sweeps across the slopes and gravity keeps deep snow from accumulating. If there is not enough snow, your kicks will hit the base surface, often rock, and possibly damage the shoe. In these instances, you may be better off removing your snowshoes and kicking in with your boots — especially if you have crampons.

Once you have mastered the toe kick, you may find yourself using it even on more moderate slopes, since it is a faster way to ascend than by using the herringbone or side step.

Side-kicking is a last-resort technique for use on very steep pitches. 1) Drive the uphill side edge of the shoe into the slope, cutting a flat step. 2-3) Now bring your back shoe around and drive its uphill edge into the slope.

TRAVERSING TECHNIQUES

The side kick is a last-resort measure, to be used when you have no choice but to traverse a steep slope. This maneuver is similar to the toe kick.

Side-kicking is a matter of driving the uphill side edge of the shoe into the slope so that the snowshoe lays flat, cutting horizontally into the grade. The problem is that most of the snowshoe is suspended out over nothing. The wider the shoe, the less effective this method is.

The side kick is an awkward motion, and it can be difficult to land the edge precisely. There is also a scary

moment when you have to bring your back shoe around and you are hanging by the edge of your front shoe. It is important to keep your

Side kicking across some steep, deep powder. Poles are a key aid to this technique.

Switchbacking reduces a steep grade into several short, less-steep sections. It's best used on the long, steep, wide-open hills so common in the West above treeline.

of the upper steps collapsing into the lower ones. It also makes the climb easier by reducing the strain that normally occurs when one foot is higher than the other for an extended period of time.

If you are doing a long traverse and have telescoping poles, you may want to shorten the uphill pole and/or lengthen the downhill pole, so that you can keep your shoulders level while maintaining good, firm pole plants. This will increase your stability, and stop you from leaning too far out over the slope (see "Learning from Rock Climbers," opposite).

SWITCHBACKING

Switchbacking is not the same thing as traversing. Traversing, or crossing a slope, is done for certain reasons: the trail you are following crosses a slope; the grade is too steep to climb so you must go across the slope; or, there is danger of an avalanche on one side of the slope and you decide to cross to the other side.

Switchbacking is an alternative route selection that effectively reduces a steep grade into several short, less-steep sections. The overall distance is greater, but easier to navigate. Switchback designs are common in road construction, especially in high-mountain passes. Cars traversing on these roads can traverse a mountain in a series of zigzags — a much easier and safer route than straight up or down.

poles securely planted at all times.

Snowshoes are not really designed to be used this way, so if possible, try to simply set the shoe down into the slope, and force your weight onto the uphill side of the shoe. This will keep the shoe flat but place more of its surface in contact with the snow.

If your shoes are short enough, it is best to traverse the slope with one step in front of the other, rather than with a normal side-by-side stride. This means breaking out only one path in the snow, rather than two side by side, thereby reducing the chance

LEARNING FROM ROCK CLIMBERS

Whether you are traversing or climbing straight up a steep slope, the natural tendency is to lean into the slope, which provides a feeling of security. Unfortunately, it's a false security.

Accomplished rock climbers know that the best angle for balancing on steep slopes is 90 degrees. When you stand straight up and down, your downward force is driven into the slope, not down the slope. The more you lean in, the more your force is pointed down the slope and the more likely it is that you will slip. On the other hand, if you overcompensate by leaning too far out, gravity will take over and pull your body down. Therefore, always try to maintain a vertical position, whether you are facing up or across a slope.

Rock climbers know that keeping the body as close to 90 degrees to the slope as possible (top) is best. When you hug the slope (bottom), your feet slip out from under you.

Switchback designs were not used in the early days of trail building. Therefore, they are much more prevalent on trails in the West, since these were built later than those in the East. In the White Mountains of New Hampshire and Maine, switchbacks are almost unheard of; and these older trails go straight up, regardless of the intensity of the slope — a fact that often surprises newcomers to these "little" mountains, who find ascents quite difficult. The fact that most eastern mountains do not ascend above treeline also limits route selection.

Jumping down steep slopes can be great fun and a welcome change of pace. Just be sure you're landing in plenty of snow free of hidden hazards.

reverse direction while standing in place.

JUMPING

Jumping is one way to get down a short, steep face, so long as you have an adequate depth of snow to land in. Whenever you jump with snowshoes, remember that the heel of the shoe will drop away, and, therefore, must be landed before the toe.

Not only can jumping on snowshoes be a quick and easy way down short slopes; it can also be fun. After a big snowfall, jumping off logs, rocks, and small mounds can provide amusement — and a change of pace — during a walk in the woods.

Switchbacks are very difficult to build in heavily forested areas, whereas in the wide-open expanses of western mountains, they are easy to build.

Switchbacking can be done on snowshoes, whether or not the trail actually switches back, as long as there is sufficient room. Try to keep the segments as steep as you can manage, so that your climbing is more like a straight fall-line ascent. This will increase the contact of your snowshoes with the surface, enable you to utilize traction devices and pivoting toe mechanisms of the snowshoes, and reduce the overall distance you'll travel.

When you reach the end of a section of climbing and are ready to switchback, use a shortened version of the kick turn (see Chapter 4) to

RUNNING
IN SHOES

Running is the area of snowshoeing that has experienced the most dramatic change due to the recent advances in snowshoe technology. Admittedly, snowshoe racing is nothing new, and running events date back to the nineteenth century. But the advantages of modern equipment have probably had more impact on running than on any other aspect of snowshoeing. Skilled snowshoers can ascend towering peaks on traditional models, right alongside others using the most advanced mountaineering models. The same is not true, however, for snowshoe runners: A competitive racer will always perform better on modern running shoes than on wooden models.

Snowshoe running can be pursued for fun, exercise, and competition. Road runners who live above the snowbelt encounter many difficulties in keeping up their fitness regimen during the winter: Roadsides are alternately slick with ice and packed snow or dirty, salty, messy slush. Road running under such conditions is unpleasant if not unsafe.

Snowshoes open up a vast new area for runners, allowing them to maintain peak condition in the heart of winter. Indeed, some proponents, myself included, believe that snowshoe running is a better workout than road running; so much so, that it

Small, lightweight modern snowshoes allow for the simple pleasure of a spontaneous family sprint, something less than pleasurable, if not impossible, on traditional wood shoes.

becomes difficult to keep up your winter level of fitness during the summer. Whichever form of running is preferred, there is little doubt that snowshoe running is superb exercise; and snow offers the added advantage of a soft surface, thus reducing wear and tear on the body.

WHERE TO GO?

For many, the hardest part of snowshoe running is not the exercise itself, but finding a suitable location, since a firm, packed surface is required. There are some races that are held in unbroken snow, especially out West. However, this is done to challenge accomplished racers. Unbroken snow is not good to regularly train on.

A packed surface serves several purposes; most important, it reduces the amount that you sink into the snow. The "rebound" off of a firm surface is also greater, which allows for flowing strides and reduces the likelihood of getting tripped up. The firm surface requires less flotation, so you can use smaller shoes that are much lighter, and don't require extra-long steps.

It can be difficult to find an uninterrupted, packed trail of any significant length. But with a little effort and creativity, you can come up with some options.

Snowmobile trails are long and

For road runners who live north of the snowbelt, snowshoe running is a godsend and arguably a *better* workout than its summertime counterpart.

Could there be a better way to let a child burn off excess energy than racing — or playing tag — on snowshoes?

will need to make sure it is okay with the snowmobilers. In many parts of the country, snowmobile clubs go to great lengths to get permission from private landowners to build trails, which they then maintain, at great expense. If they decide to prohibit other users, you must respect their wishes.

If you are allowed to use the trails, always be alert, and when a snowmobile approaches, stop running and get off the trail. Do not just move to the side, but actually leave the trail, both for your safety and that of the snowmobiler, who may try to stop suddenly upon seeing you in the trail. Fortunately, it is relatively easy to determine when snowmobiles are coming, as they are not very stealthy.

Nordic centers that offer skating trails are another good choice, assuming they allow snowshoers. Never use cross-country trails that

firmly packed. If you have them in your area, this can be a good place to run, with certain caveats. First, you

THE STOWE RECREATION PATH

The town of Stowe, Vermont, has a rich history of outdoor recreation, especially in winter. Home to one of the oldest and most famous Alpine ski areas in the country, Stowe is also the destination of choice for many Nordic skiers and snowshoers. There are several well-known cross-country centers

in town, including the internationally famed Trapp Family Lodge, founded by the family featured in the movie, *The Sound of Music*. Stowe's Nordic ski areas interconnect, offering many miles of trails; almost all now cater to the needs of snowshoers as well as skiers.

One of the most unique features of the town is the recreation path, a marvel that draws annual visits from urban planners all over

have been tracked, as your footprints will ruin the tracks for skiers. Skating trails, on the other hand, are packed, so you won't usually damage the trail's surface.

As snowshoeing has grown in popularity, many Nordic centers have embraced the sport, offering rentals, lessons, and even special trails designated for snowshoeing. Perhaps soon they will also offer groomed, packed running trails for snowshoe racing and training.

If you have your own land and a snowmobile, you can pack a trail to whatever dimensions suit you, although relatively few snowshoers enjoy the luxury of this option. If you have a friend with a snowmobile who can come over and pack it for you, you're in business. You can make a smaller loop on your own, either by pulling a weighted sled, or simply by running around the unpacked loop

A firmly packed surface is best for regular training. Ask to use snowmobilers' trails or cross-country ski trails groomed for skating.

the world. This paved path runs parallel to the Mountain Road, from downtown Stowe to the base of the Alpine ski area, a distance of several miles. Along the way, it crosses several beautiful bridges, and there are benches strategically placed for rest breaks. The path goes by many of the town's best restaurants, and it is not at all unusual for visitors to park their skis or snowshoes at the door and enjoy lunch. There are several rental outfitters along the path, supplying sports equipment year-round. In the winter the path is used primarily by cross-country skiers and snowshoers, and in the summer by joggers, walkers, in-line skaters, and bikers. Stowe is also home to Tubbs Snowshoe Company, the nation's largest snowshoe manufacturer.

several times, just as you would on an oval running track at a gym or outdoor field. Consider this activity part of your training regimen. Even better, see if you can recruit a handful of other snowshoers to help out.

Many golf courses are open to skiers, snowshoers, and sledders in the winter, and often you can make your own running loop out on the course. You will have to repack the loop every time it snows, but if you have a local group of snowshoe-running enthusiasts, this is no big deal.

A few communities maintain trails that are suitable for running, such as the renowned Stowe Recreation Trail in Stowe, Vermont (see "The Stowe Recreation Path," page 92), but these are few and far between. If you are lucky enough to live near one of these trails, you are a perfect candidate for a pair of running snowshoes.

STRIDE AND RHYTHM

Running on snowshoes is more tiring than road running. You must carry the added weight of your snowshoes, and usually, heavier footwear as well. In addition, more energy is absorbed by snow than would be by a paved or packed dirt surface, and there is much less rebound than on a paved surface. If you have ever run along the beach, you can understand just how exhausting this can be. Take all of this into account when you go out

running on snowshoes for the first time. Set your sights a little lower than you would for a regular run — if you normally do five miles, for instance, you might want to try just three on snowshoes.

You should be comfortable with basic snowshoeing skills, and also have some experience running on dry land before attempting snowshoe running. There is no great mystery to it, but it does require concentration and coordination.

When you run on snowshoes, try to get into a smooth stride, with each foot traveling the same distance on every step, just as you would on the road. This will help alleviate any tendency to step on one shoe with the other. Many racing snowshoes are asymmetrical, with the bindings closer to the inside edge, so you can keep your feet closer together and use a tighter, more normal stride. If your strides are not consistent, you will have to devote more thought to being careful about where you place your feet. Also, try not to raise your knees as high as you would on the road. The added weight on your feet will affect you more the higher you lift them off the ground.

Snowshoe running requires more concentration than road running. Even on a groomed, packed trail, the surface is probably more varied than you are used to on the road. Patches of snow in the sun or shade may be wetter and heavier, or alternatively, harder and slicker, so traction is always an issue. Be prepared for some minor slippage, and expect to occasionally sink an extra inch or two.

Snowshoes also have "flop," which occurs because the heel of the snowshoe drops away with every step, and then your own heel comes down and strikes the deck of the snowshoe. When running, this continual flopping can be

Be prepared for the constant flopping of snowshoes when running. To minimize flopping, choose limited-rotation bindings (see Chapter 2).

annoying at first, but you'll quickly learn to live with it. The design of the shoe and binding greatly affect the amount of flop you experience, so when buying running models, this is an important factor to consider. If you do not enjoy running in your snowshoes, they will end up sitting in your garage all winter, so, again, try before you buy.

Since you do not sink much on packed trails, waterproof shoes are not necessary. Many runners use conventional running shoes (often adding gaiters), because they are comfortable, cushioned, and light. This is

fine, as long as you are warm enough. For additional support and protection from the elements, you may want to try shoes that are made for trail running. Trail-running shoes have become increasingly popular for snowshoeing because they combine the fit characteristics of running shoes with the increased support and water resistance of hiking boots.

Some racers permanently mount running shoes to their bindings. By bolting the bottom of the sneaker to the snowshoe, you get consistent attachment, and can further reduce the weight you are carrying by elimi-

Where the powder is deep but also dry and light, groomed trails are not a prerequisite of running.

nating the straps and other parts of the binding. Most snowshoes are not designed for this modification, so you have to be somewhat handy and improvise. If you put bolts through the soles of the sneakers, remove the "footbeds" first. After replacing them, you may find that you still have to insert additional foam liners to protect your feet from the heads of the bolts or rivets.

During shorter races or sprints, many snowshoe racers do not use poles, since the trail surface is fairly uniform, and experience enables them to balance well. Freed from carrying poles, racers are able to use more "arm drive" while running. However, during longer endurance events or hill-climbing races, they often find that the use of poles is advantageous.

TRAINING

Training with snowshoes is not much different than with sneakers, but there are a few unique considerations. Your speed will be slower, so don't be disappointed if you can't average the same number of minutes per mile. It's a good idea to clock your times and find out how your snowshoe running speed compares with your road running speed. This way you will be able to tell when you are improving. Unfortunately, it can be hard to measure trail distances, since most pedometers are not very accurate. On the road, runners can simply clock distances with their car odometers, but this is not an option on a snowy trail. Therefore, many runners train by time, rather than by distance.

In all sports, muscle balance is important; when two muscles that perform opposite functions develop differently, it puts the weaker one in danger of damage. Your quadriceps — the large muscle in the front of your thigh —

Snowshoe manufacturers sponsor many events, usually 5- and 10-kilometer races. Ask a local outfitter about events scheduled in your area.

extends the lower leg, while your hamstring — the large muscle in the back of your thigh — retracts it. If you run on snowshoes frequently, you will strengthen your quadriceps disproportionately, because they are lifting the added weight of the shoes. To maintain muscle balance it's a good idea to do some strength-training exercises for your hamstrings

using weights. This will help to prevent injuries.

Tom Sobal, the most successful snowshoe racer in the world, trains year-round in Leadville, Colorado (see "Snowshoeing's Edwin Moses?," page 98). For keeping in shape in the "off-season" he suggests that "the most important thing to do is maintain aerobic fitness, by hiking,

While snowshoe races are becoming more numerous and more serious, the absence of big prize money ensures that everyone is there for a good time.

RACING

There has been a remarkable proliferation of organized snowshoe races in the last few years. Whereas most races were once held in conjunction with snowshoe festivals, many are now stand-alone events that participants travel significant distances to

running, or mountain biking over the same terrain you would snowshoe on."

SNOWSHOEING'S EDWIN MOSES?

Track and field legend Edwin Moses's total domination of his sport — hurdles — has led to his name being synonymous with winning and winning often. To be referred to as a sport's Edwin Moses is a high compliment, reserved for those rarefied individuals who completely dominate their field.

There is such a man in the field of snowshoe racing, and his name is Tom Sobal. Sobal, a resident of Leadville, Colorado, doesn't just win the occasional race; he wins them all, over any distance.

He has run sub-three-hour marathons in the snow, a feat few serious runners can emulate on dry

land under the best of conditions. He wins 5-Ks, 10-Ks, and 100-mile races regularly, counting his losses on his fingers. Race promoter Andrew Bielecki's strange choice of surface and the desert heat didn't stop Sobal from running far ahead of the field, and achieving his 5-kilometer course best of 23:14, during the 1995 Extreme Heat Snowshoe race held at Great Sand Dunes National Monument in Colorado.

Colorado's *Summit County Journal* wrote that Sobal "has a reputation for winning just about every snowshoe race he enters." *Sports Illustrated* pulled no punches, stating that "when he has a pair of snowshoes strapped to his feet, no other snowshoe racer in the country can run faster."

get to. A large part of the credit for the increase in snowshoe races goes to manufacturers, who use them as marketing tools to demonstrate and sell their shoes, and to get more people involved in the sport. Tubbs, Redfeather, Sherpa, and Atlas have all sponsored extensive race series, in which competitors can enter multiple races and accrue points toward season championships. By holding multiple

Events come in many different forms, from this race on Lake Placid in the Adirondacks to the Mount Elbert Race up the highest peak in Colorado.

events, these series increase the likelihood that some races will be held near you.

Tom Sobal's wife, Melissa, also a successful racer, competes regularly at events all across the country. According to Melissa, "races have become much more popular, especially out here [she lives in Leadville, Colorado]. It's not unusual these days

to see 400 competitors at a race."

In addition to snowshoe manufacturers, many large retailers, such as EMS and L.L. Bean, host snowshoe events, as do many ski resorts. *Snowshoer* magazine (see Sources & Resources) publishes an up-to-date national calendar of events. Event calendars are also available from equipment manufacturers, and many sporting goods stores post information for local events. The easiest way to find out about races is to contact a snowshoe manufacturer who is located in your part of the country.

The increased interest in racing has given rise to an increase in the variety of events offered. Races now cover almost every conceivable distance, from 100-yard sprints to the 100-mile Ididashoe in Alaska. The most common race lengths are 5 and 10 kilometers, but marathons and grueling mountain ascents are popular, as well.

While snowshoe races have become more serious, the absence of big prize money ensures that most competitors are there for camaraderie and a good time. Many events feature post-race parties, complete with beer and barbecues, and often there are a lot of door prizes given away to a limited field of competitors. Snowshoe racing is one of the few sports where you have a reasonable chance of winning something just for showing up!

Some of the biggest annual events are the Snowshoe to the Great White North race series held throughout Colorado, and the Tubbs 10-K series. The Mount Elbert Snowshoe Race up the highest peak in Colorado is a prestigious — and grueling — annual event, considered by many in the snowshoe community to be the most important race of the year. Manufacturers often send sponsored teams to compete.

Many events feature more than one race, so to start out, you can choose a distance you feel comfortable with. Some even provide use of snowshoes during the race, so if you are an avid snowshoer who doesn't own a pair of running shoes, this is an economical way to give them a try.

BACKCOUNTRY SKILLS

T he word backcountry conjures up different images for different people. To some, any hike off the beaten path is a backcountry adventure; while for hard-core mountaineers, backcountry refers to an area filled with ice climbs, untracked bowls, and winter camping.

The goal of a backcountry trek is usually the same for both groups: to get away from it all. The thing to remember when you get away is that eventually you want to get back, preferably unharmed.

There are dangers even on well-traveled trails in summer, but winter brings with it many additional hazards. Once you step off that trail into

the backcountry, these dangers multiply at a rapid rate. Backcountry travel, even on a day trip, is not for the inexperienced, and requires advanced skills and additional equipment.

If you are unfamiliar with the techniques outlined in this chapter, and are not going to be with people who have backcountry snowshoeing experience, your best bet is to take an organized trip or course, or hire a guide. Outdoor retailers like REI and EMS offer courses in winter camping, climbing, survival, navigation, and other related topics. Outdoor schools like the National Outdoor Leadership School (NOLS), Outward Bound, the

Athabaska River Valley, Jasper National Park, Alberta, Canada. It's vital to get instruction in map and compass navigation and wilderness first aid before venturing into such country.

American Alpine Institute, Exum Mountaineering, International Mountain Equipment, and many others teach the required skills and offer group trips with experienced leaders (see Sources & Resources for more information).

Many colleges and universities also have outing clubs that offer instruction and leadership, as do regional hiking associations such as the Green Mountain Club, the Colorado Mountain Club, and the Appalachian Mountain Club. Finally, outfitters near popular expedition sites offer group trips and private guides. One of the most popular mountaineering destinations in the country is Washington's Mount Ranier, and there are numerous qualified outfitters in the region. Other popular destinations with good local outfitters include Grand Teton, Wyoming; Mount Washington, New Hampshire; and Mount Hood, Oregon.

I cannot overemphasize the need for qualified instruction. The rest of this chapter discusses skills that you will need to snowshoe in the backcountry; however, there is no substitute for hands-on learning.

NAVIGATION

Route-finding is much more difficult in the winter than the summer. A well-used hiking trail is easy to follow when thousands of footsteps are worn into the soil, or the footpath is two feet wide and absent of vegetation. Cover this path with even an inch of snow, and every indication that it was ever there vanishes.

In many parts of the country, most of the trees lose their leaves in winter, and vegetation recedes. What was once a clear pathway through thick foliage is now just one of many avenues through the brush. Even a trail that you are very familiar with can "disappear" quickly once the leaves have fallen.

Practice map reading on well-marked dayhikes so that when you need one, you have the skill to use it. Arriving at consensus minimizes error.

Snowshoers love deep snow, since a good base is necessary to cover rocks, roots, and other obstacles. A good base can also completely obscure blazes, the marks painted on trees to show where the trail goes. Think about the typical blaze on a hiking trail. How high is it off the ground? Four feet? Five feet? In snow country, especially in the mountains, it is common to get this much snow; afterward the last remaining trail markings are gone. Above tree-line, many trails are marked with cairns — small man-made rock piles, usually less than three feet high. At altitudes at which cairns are popular, this amount of snow falls regularly, and quickly buries these landmarks.

Proper navigation in winter or summer requires the ability to use a map and compass. Make sure you use a good compass, as well as a detailed map of the area you are visiting. A page from a guidebook that describes the trail in mile-long sections will not suffice. Other maps, such as those provided by parks or local clubs may be helpful,

Don't go into the backcountry without USGS topographic maps, a good compass, and the know-how to accurately use them.

A snowshoer in northern Utah's Wasatch Range pauses to consult his topographic map.

Sources & Resources.)

The best way to become proficient in reading maps is to use them when you don't have to. Try this on summer hikes over familiar terrain. Practice will prepare you for the idiosyncrasies of map reading before your life depends on it.

Using a compass is not difficult in practice, but without one in your hand, the theory is difficult to grasp. The arrow on your compass always points to magnetic north, which unfortunately, is not the same as true north. This is because there is a difference of hundreds of miles between the true North Pole and magnetic North Pole. The angular difference between the two is called variation. The amount and direction of variation is affected by your geographic location in respect to true north and magnetic north.

Although compasses always point to magnetic north, maps are always based on true north. This is not as big a problem as it sounds,

but they are often out-of-date or lacking in sufficient detail to be of assistance once you become lost.

For winter hiking, a detailed topographical map is best. United States Geological Survey (USGS) maps are available for every state, and are excellent, but for large areas you may need several due to their detailed scale. Private companies, such as Trails Illustrated, make some excellent maps for popular adventure destinations, such as many national parks and forests. (A great resource for obtaining maps to all areas within the United States, as well as destinations around the world, is Adventurous Traveler Bookstore — see

however, because the variation for a given region should always be printed on your map. Therefore, if you determine a "true" course from your map, and want to know what compass course to follow, all you need to do is add or subtract the variation given on the map.

If you know where you are on the map, you can get a "bearing" on a distant landmark that you wish to head toward by pointing the compass at the object, and taking a reading. You can then use that compass reading to remain on the right path. This is both easier and more difficult than it sounds. If you are accustomed to navigating by compass, an occa-sional glance at the needle will keep you on course. If this is your first time, most likely you will stop frequently and second guess each reading. However, with practice, you can become efficient at using a compass in no time at all.

The best way to learn is to take a course, since it's very much a hands-on experience. If you believe you have some innate navigational ability, you can try to learn from a book. The classic orienteering tome, *Be An Expert With Map and Compass*, can be found at most bookstores. However, to be safe and properly prepared, always carry a compass and make sure you are comfortable using it.

GPS

The Global Positioning System (GPS) is a techno-logical break-through that allows you to determine your position from anywhere in the world. GPS is currently com-prised of 24 satel-lites orbiting the earth at a distance of 12,000 miles. Each satel-lite contains two atomic clocks, accurate to within one second every 70,000 years. A handheld GPS receiver calculates the coor-dinates (longitude and latitude) of your position by taking a reading from three or more of these satel-lites. Depending on the cost of your unit, accuracy can be any-where from 100 meters to less than one meter from your actual position.

Handheld GPS receivers do far more than just tell you your coordinates, however. They allow you to store reference points along

continued on page 106

GPS
continued from page 105

the way, sometimes hundreds, and calculate routes back to and between these points. For example, you can take a GPS reading when you park your car and enter it into the receiver's memory. Your GPS unit will then be able to lead you back to your car, with arrows and distances, from any point on earth!

Theoretically, GPS makes getting lost impossible. I say theoretically, because of course there are exceptions. At times, physical conditions, such as trees or other obstructions, can make it impossible to get a reading. Additionally, GPS is an electronic device, and electronic devices are prone to failure in the wilderness, either from damage or from something as simple and common as the bat-

teries running out. Batteries do not work nearly as well in the cold, and even under the best of circumstances, GPS receivers do not have a long life with a single set of batteries. To preserve the batteries, it helps to carry your receiver inside your jacket in the winter.

Despite these drawbacks, GPS is a remarkable tool that should be part of every outdoor person's equipment. Affordable GPS receiver units that are small enough for hikers and snowshoers to carry, have recently been introduced. Handheld units the size of a television remote control cost less than $200 and weigh under 10 ounces. While GPS is not a substitute for knowing how to use a map and compass, it can save your life, and is undeniably useful in white-out conditions, when you cannot see any landmarks.

CROSSING ICE

One of the problems with crossing ice in the backcountry is that you might not even know it's there. If you're following a trail through fairly open terrain and it crosses a stream, you may never even see it. Worse, you may come to the edge of a "clearing" and cross it, not knowing that it is a actually a pond.

The only solution is to use cau-

tion and common sense, and keep on the lookout for anything out of the ordinary. Ponds are completely flat, whereas fields rarely are. Trails that cross streams usually slope down toward the streams and up from them. Being able to "read" the terrain will be your best defense against surprises. In addition, it is always best to be prepared, so bring along useful equipment, such as traction aids and rope.

Approach all ice crossings with extreme caution, feeling your way slowly to find the safest route. Ice bridges across streams pose particular hazards, because the thickness of the ice can be unpredictable.

A minimum of two inches of "good" ice is recommended to support a human being. Unfortunately, it is often difficult to determine when ice is safe. Given the choice, it is best to avoid ice crossings altogether. Many times, however, this is not possible. If you encounter ice during a backcountry outing, there are several steps to follow, in order to ensure a safe crossing.

Before setting out on the ice, test the surface as best you can with a stick or pole. If you strike it and it makes a hollow noise, that can indicate that there is air trapped just below the surface, which means the ice is not safe to cross. Thick ice will sound a reassuring clunk! Also look for gray spots in the ice where water

may be seeping up. These are weak spots and should be avoided.

Look around the perimeter of the body of water and see if you can locate a stream feeding into it or out of it. You may actually see moving water, or just a clear path, free from vegetation heading out into the woods from the edge of the pond or lake. If you find a stream, cross the ice as far from that point as possible, since the area around moving water is less likely to freeze securely. When traveling over ice in groups, stay far apart, at least 20 feet. This keeps the weight of your group spread out over a broader area.

Snowshoes have several features that are helpful when traveling over ice. They have traction aids, which

Icy, wind-blown summit in New Hampshire's White Mountains. Above treeline snow conditions can change dramatically, and crampons may be a welcome addition to your gear.

can be invaluable on slippery ice, and they distribute your weight over a much larger area, thus reducing the chance of breaking through. The one drawback is that if you do fall through, snowshoes can greatly hinder your efforts to get back out. For that reason, always loosen your bindings before setting out onto the ice, so that in the event of a mishap, you can kick your shoes loose. Finally, if you have a reasonable expectation of encountering ice crossings on your trip, bring a 30-foot length of rope with you.

If you have poles with you, hold them across your body as you cross the ice. Then, if you do fall through, the ends of the poles may support you on the edge of the hole, and assist you in climbing out.

If you do fall through, don't panic. Try to kick with your legs and push with your arms to launch yourself as far out of the water as possible and onto the surrounding ice. As soon as you make contact, continue to roll, slide, or wiggle away from the hole. Get as far as you can from the weak edge as quickly as possible. If the ice around the hole will not support you, keep breaking it with your hands and body until you either reach shore or thicker ice.

When traveling in a group, cross the ice single file, so that the leader can determine whether the ice is safe. Make sure you use your rope to tie off the leader, so that if he or she falls through, the other members of the party can pull him or her out.

In the event that you (or a member of your group) has fallen through ice, it is of utmost importance that you get dry and warm as quickly as possible to avoid the risk of hypothermia (see "Hypothermia," page 115). Borrow dry clothes or get to the nearest shelter — fast! The consequences of falling through ice are very serious; therefore, always cross ice with extreme caution.

Be mindful when planning a backcountry trip to take into account the additional weight of winter gear when selecting snowshoes (see "Winter Weight Gain," page 26).

SELF ARREST
With an Ice Ax

It is helpful to carry an ice ax while snowshoeing in the backcountry, so that you can perform "self arrest" in the event that you slip and begin to slide down a slope. This skill is not difficult to learn, but practice is necessary to master it.

To perform self arrest, as you fall, position the ax diagonally across your chest, gripping the end of the shaft with one hand and the shaft just below the ax head (at the throat) with the other. If you slip and start to slide on your back immediately flip to your stomach and dig the ax point into the snow or ice.

The key to a successful self arrest is to remain calm, but act very quickly. Your sliding body will accelerate rapidly, and the faster you are going the less likely you will succeed in stopping.

Without an Ice Ax

Many snowshoers do not own an ice ax and do not anticipate sliding dangerously during an outing. This is a perfectly reasonable assumption. Nonetheless, it can happen, and it is possible that you may someday find yourself sliding down a slope and wish to stop. The best way to slide is to get onto your stomach immediately, with your feet pointed downhill. This may seem strange, since riding on your buttocks seems to offer more

For many, a hut-to-hut tour is a good balance between experiencing the backcountry and having to take full responsibility for winter survival.

Backcountry expeditions often require more gear than can be reasonably carried on your back. This is especially true on longer trips. In general, winter camping requires a lot more equipment than summer trips. Since snow is slick, one method of carrying a load is to pull a sled. You can carry more than twice the weight in a sled than you can on your back with the same amount of effort.

The sled should be plastic and flat bottomed without runners. It can be a relatively inexpensive model, but you need to devise a method to attach it to your body. Do not consider the usual method of pulling the sled by hand with a rope — it will tire you out and prevent you from using your poles effectively. Instead, loop the rope of the sled around your waist, or better yet, employ two rigid support rods on either side of your hips, with a rope or strap that crosses your middle and connects them. This system will track much better and keep the sled from fishtailing. It will also make it easier to control the sled when going downhill, by keeping it a

control, but it is easier to stop when you are face down. To do so, you need to increase your drag and dig into the snow as much as possible. By being on your stomach, you can push your fingers deep into the surface and raise your upper body to get a lot of weight on your hands. At the same time, spread your legs, turn your toes outward, and dig the inside edges of your snowshoes into the slope. By making a "V" with your legs, you are using a technique similar to the herringbone step. By turning your toes out and deploying the edges of your snowshoes, you are creating a much wider surface area across the slope. Both of these tricks will arrest your slide.

If you have poles, hold them across the slope in your hands, and when you dig your fingers into the slope, the poles will act as an added brake.

fixed distance behind you. There are small sleds, called pulks, that are made especially for mountaineering trips, and are equipped with good poles and harnesses. Many snowshoers, however, make do with a homemade alternative.

Sleds are best suited to wide-open expanses and gentle rolling hills, but are difficult to manage up and down steep slopes. In the Northeast, where the trails are narrow, the woods are dense, and almost everything is below treeline, a sled may be impossible to handle when negotiating tight stretches.

On multi-day trips, you may be able to haul the sled to a base camp. Then, on shorter hikes, you can take only what you need, and return to camp to resupply. This method is especially useful if you are snowshoeing deep into the wilderness to

A small sled, called a pulk, is an ideal way to carry the extra gear and clothing that winter expeditions require.

A SLIPPERY SITUATION

While winter camping in the Green Mountains last winter, my friend and I found the trail above treeline difficult to follow as it switched back toward the ridge. We knew that the trail then turned and followed the ridge line, so we decided to take the straightest route up to the top of the ridge where we could then intercept the trail.

As my friend began to climb up the chute we had chosen, he wisely stuck to the left-hand side, where some small evergreens lined the edge. I stopped to take some pictures and did not take note of his ascent route.

I began climbing moments later, charging straight up the middle of the chute where the snow was the least stable. I was

continued on page 112

A SLIPPERY SITUATION
continued from page 111

testing a new pair of technical backcountry snowshoes on this trip and wanted to put them to the test and see how well they performed. Since avalanches were rare in this region, I was not worried.

The shoes had great traction, and I made it two-thirds of the way up the chute with little difficulty. Suddenly, the snow broke out around the steps I was toe-kicking into the slope and I began to slide backward, the crust of the slope crumbling under me. I dug my hands and feet in to increase my drag, and quickly arrested my slide. That's when my real troubles began.

I looked around and surveyed my options. There was no way I could move up, and down was not a better choice. The slightest movement of my feet would continue my slide, toward the bottom of the chute and the trees and rocks 200 feet below. I finally decided my only option was to traverse the slope, and head for the safety of the small evergreens.

Facing the slope and punching both fists deep into the snow, I anchored my arms, then gingerly lifted my left foot, swung it as far to the left as I could, and toe-kicked into the slope. I waited a moment for the snow to consolidate under my weight, then repeated the motion with my right foot. I then repositioned each arm and began again. Moving 12 inches at a time, I made my way across the chute, maybe 40 feet in all, never moving one limb until the other three were well planted. It was with great relief that I grasped the first tree branch.

---

the base of a peak, which you then plan to ascend.

To make the sled run with less resistance, lubricate the bottom. Most ski shops sell wipe-on disposable applications for increasing the speed of Alpine skis; these will work well on most sleds.

If you do tow a sled, make sure it is securely fastened to avoid runaways, and always bring extra rope.

Then, if you reach a short pitch or unexpected steep, rough section, you can belay the sled, or ascend first and then tow it up hand over hand. A 200-foot length of quality mountaineering rope will make little weight difference in your load, but will make a big difference in your ability to maneuver the sled.

WINTER SAFETY

Some novice adventurers trek into the woods full of bravado, but lacking adequate clothing, equipment, and knowledge. Somehow, they manage to return on schedule and unscathed. These winter enthusiasts journey out time and again, year after year, without incident. They are lucky. Although winter is a wonderful season, rich in opportunities for unlimited exploration and adventure, it is also a season of severe, and many times unpredictable, weather. While winter's dangers should not prevent you from enjoying nature's secret season, they are very real, and deserving of respect. Knowledge, experience, and pre-paredness are the keys to enjoying winter activities safely.

WEATHER

The rule of thumb in regard to winter weather is simple: expect the unexpected. No matter how "bad" the weather, if you knew what is was going to be, with certainty, you could prepare for it. The problem is that you never know, and once you consider how uncertain weather reports are, you won't want to bet your well-being on them.

Weather conditions change quickly in the winter — especially in the mountains — and whiteouts,

Weather conditions change rapidly and vary wildly in winter, especially in the far north and at high altitudes. You must not venture into such regions without being fully prepared for the worst conditions possible.

pared for such changes. Remember that injuries like frostbite, snow blindness, and other winter calamities occur to Alpine skiers frequently, when they are never more than a few minutes from shelter.

Another concern in the winter is the short amount of time needed for something to go wrong. If your toes or earlobes begin to hurt from the cold, you start to shiver

windstorms, and large decreases or increases in temperature are common. When journeying any distance into the wild, you must be pre-

THE TRAGEDY ON EVEREST

The tragedy on Mount Everest in May of 1996 is widely regarded as one of the worst in the annals of mountaineering. Eight individuals from two different expeditions died on the mountain, including two of the most respected and experienced mountain guides in the world. While it will probably never be fully known what role judgment played in the incident, it is an ugly reminder that even the most experienced outdoor travelers can't always prepare for Mother Nature's worst. What is known is that the combined effects of altitude, a sudden storm at the summit, low temperatures, and wind chills below -100°F were the major contributing factors to the tragedy.

Himalayan expeditions, and other high-peak efforts are often at the mercy of the weather, and it is not unusual for expeditions to be "trapped" in tents for weeks waiting for the elements to cooperate.

Even in fairly familiar terrain closer to home, winter weather conditions, such as whiteouts, can be disorienting. And winter conditions can be unforgiving of even minor mistakes.

uncontrollably, or, worst of all, you fall in water, reaction time to prevent serious injury may be only minutes. If you are 10 miles from the nearest shelter, you need to know what to do.

HYPOTHERMIA

Hypothermia is the most insidious of winter ailments. Unlike frostbite, it comes on without telltale pain, and can and often does occur at temperatures as high as 50°F. Worse, it is very serious and if untreated can quickly lead to death.

Simply put, hypothermia occurs when the body is no longer able to maintain a temperature of approximately 98.6°F. There are several ways in which the body loses heat (see "Five Causes of Cold," page 117). Hypothermia is also known as exposure, and this adequately describes two of the primary culprits — wind and rain. One of the reasons why hypothermia is the most dangerous outdoor safety threat is that the temperatures at which it occurs can be found all year long; summer hikers succumb to hypothermia as frequently as skiers and snowshoers. In warmer conditions, people tend to wear and carry less clothing, putting themselves at greater risk.

Small children are especially vulnerable to hypothermia. Never assume they are warm enough and take frequent snack breaks.

During activity, the body generates heat. The purpose of wearing appropriate winter clothing (see Chapter 9) is to conserve that heat, prevent radiation loss, and protect the skin from conductive and convective losses, while getting rid of moisture. To prevent hypothermia, it's key to avoid exposing skin to the elements.

Another cause of hypothermia is dehydration. Like any other outdoor sport, snowshoeing requires drinking large amounts of water — several quarts per day. It is often said that dehydration is a more serious problem in the winter than in the summer; without the sweaty, over-heated feeling that occurs during summer activities, you may not feel the need to drink. Nonetheless, if you wait until you are thirsty, you are already suffering from mild dehydration.

Ample food is important as well. As far as your body is concerned, food is fuel, and fuel is burned to generate heat. Inadequate fluid and caloric intake ranks second to cold, wind, and rain as causes of hypothermia.

Hypothermia is easy to diagnose. The afflicted person shivers uncontrollably, has impaired speech and coordination, and a lowered body temperature. A classic sign is sudden exhaustion, which is the reason why the final act of many doomed expeditioners is to take a nap. The urge to sleep becomes extremely pronounced.

Unfortunately, hypothermia victims often resist treatment, because they are unable to think clearly. Still, they must be rewarmed quickly. If their clothes are wet, change them into dry clothes, get them into a sleeping bag, and if possible, shelter them from the elements. Because they are already chilled, the insulation of the clothes and sleeping bag will not be completely effective, since they cannot generate as much body heat as before. For mild hypothermia, where the core body temperature is still above 90°F, rewarming with external heat, such as warm water bottles or a companion's body heat, is recommended.

For severe hypothermia, where body heat drops below 90°F, the individual should not be rewarmed, since cold blood from the extremities, after being warmed, returns to the heart, and can cause cardiac arrest. In cases of severe hypothermia, the person must be transported to a hospital. Once wrapped up, severely hypothermic patients can remain stable for up to 15 hours during transport.

FIVE CAUSES OF COLD

There are five ways in which the human body loses heat.

CONDUCTION
The transfer of heat from warmer to cooler objects. The larger the temperature difference, the greater the rate of heat flow. This is why your ears get warmer when you put your hands over them. It is also why you can get cold from sitting in the snow. Direct contact with the ground or snow is the most common cause of conductive loss.

CONVECTION
Heat loss that occurs when cooler air moves across exposed skin. While wind chill has no effect on inanimate objects like a glass of water, it has a very real effect on living tissue. The colder the air is and the faster it is moving, the more pronounced the effect.

RADIATION
Infrared heat waves emanating from the body through uncovered skin. All physical substances, no matter what their temperature, radiate energy in waves. The hotter the object, the greater the radiation. In the summer, your body's radiation keeps you cool; in the winter, however, it can make you quite cold.

EVAPORATION
Your body's attempt to turn any moisture on the surface of your skin into vapor. The moisture can be perspiration, or an outside source of water, such as rain. The process of evaporation requires a lot of energy which translates into heat loss.

RESPIRATION
The act of inhaling and exhaling air. When you breathe, you inhale cold air, which is then warmed inside your lungs. When you exhale, this heat is lost.

Hypothermia can strike when conditions seem benign and you least expect it. Be sure to drink plenty of water and eat high-calorie snacks.

Since treatment of hypothermia is difficult and often unsuccessful, consider prevention to be the number one treatment. Make sure that you dress appropriately, bring extra clothing, and eat and drink adequate amounts of food and liquid when venturing out into the winter wilderness.

FROSTBITE

Frostbite is the freezing of body tissue. It most often affects the hands and feet, as well as the cheeks, nose, and ears. The extremities are vulnerable because they have a large surface area relative to their volume and circulation, and therefore lose heat to radiation, conduction, evaporation, and convection more quickly.

Superficial frostbite is often associated with a tingling feeling, and inspection may reveal the skin to be gray, white, or yellowish, and hard to the touch. You can rewarm such parts by covering them with your hands, or in the case of fingers, sticking them in your armpits. Do not rewarm at temperatures above 98.6°F (e.g., by sticking the affected part in hot water). While there is usually no permanent damage associated with superficial frostbite, affected parts may be susceptible to refreezing, which can cause real damage, so after rewarming, take immediate and appropriate measures to protect yourself from the cold.

Severe frostbite is much more serious. Also known as deep frostbite, it is when there is solid freezing of tissues. The amount of permanent damage sustained (or the necessity of amputation) depends on how much of a temperature drop occurred and how long the tissue was frozen. For this reason, rewarming should be done quickly, by immersing the body part in water between 102 and 108°F. Only rewarm if medical evaluation will be delayed for hours, and if you can *guarantee* against refreezing.

ALTITUDE SICKNESS AND ACUTE MOUNTAIN SICKNESS

Altitude sickness usually occurs at elevations of 8,000 feet or higher, although the elevation is not as important as the speed of one's ascent. The absence of proper acclimation to higher altitudes is usually the culprit. It is recommended that at 8,000 feet or higher, ascent from one night's sleep to the next be limited to 1,000 feet. During the intervening days you may hike higher so long as you come down to sleep. In a nutshell: hike high, sleep low.

There are many readily accessible snowshoe trips that venture above 8,000 feet; the potential for altitude sickness during these trips is a real concern. At 10,000 feet, oxygen pressure drops to two-thirds

THE WORLD'S WORST WEATHER

Many people are surprised to find that they do not have to journey to Tibet or Antarctica to expose themselves to truly dangerous winter conditions. Even the most benign mountain ranges claim lives each year, and despite it's well-earned reputation as the most dangerous small mountain in the world, one in particular is continuously underestimated.

I have ascended New Hampshire's Mount Washington several times, in summer and winter conditions, although sometimes it is hard to tell the difference. I have passed hikers on warm July days making their way up in tennis shoes, shorts, and T-shirts, with no supplies, apparently unaware of the drastic changes that await them during the three-hour ascent,

which is not technically difficult. Perhaps this is why the mountain, despite numerous warnings, claims lives each year, and in every season.

The weather station atop the peak has the dubious distinction of honor of being located at the focal point of the "world's worst weather." At 6,288 feet the summit is low by serious climbing standards — it is not even the highest mountain in the eastern United States, and is downright paltry when compared with the Rockies. But to those caught above treeline in the exposed rock fields of Mount Washington, when hurricane-force winds rip across the summit, as they do one out of every three days, height is the least of their concerns.

Extreme winter-like condi-

continued on page 120

THE WORLD'S WORST WEATHER
continued from page 119

tions can be found at Mount Washington any time of year, and wind speeds of over 100 miles an hour have been recorded in every single month. The highest wind speed ever recorded on the surface of the earth, an unbelievable 231 miles per hour, swept across the summit on April 12, 1934. The most significant snow accumulation in the history of the United States for a one-day period, an amazing 49.3 inches, was recorded on Mount Washington. The record low temperature at the summit was a bone-chilling -46°F without the wind chill.

But what makes Mount Washington so dangerous is that the temperature there is often not below freezing. Temperatures in the 30s and 40s (which are the norm), coupled with the frequent rains and driving winds, are often far more serious than colder tem-

peratures. Rain and wind combine to make it almost impossible to stay dry, and hypothermia becomes more of an issue than it would be at lower temperatures when it would not be as moist out.

New Hampshire's White Mountains produce life-threatening winter weather.

One of the most popular ascents of Mount Washington is through Tuckerman's Ravine, reached by a relatively easy trail through dense woods. Last September, fooled by the promise of an Indian summer day, we set out to hike this well-worn route. Emerging from the woods into the windswept ravine just above treeline, our group went from being warm to bitterly cold in less than five minutes. Fortunately, we relied on our judgment, considered our options, and analyzed our equipment before coming up with a new strategy — turning around.

of that available at sea level, and at 18,000 feet it drops to one-third.

Symptoms of altitude sickness include fatigue, weakness, headaches, nausea, vomiting, and shortness of breath. These can be hard to distinguish from other ills of winter exertion, but if you are at a high altitude, be suspect and assume that these symptoms are indicative of altitude sickness.

Acclimation is the key to preventing altitude sickness: Do not camp more than 1,000 feet higher than you did the previous night.

If you begin to experience symptoms of altitude sickness, you can try to stay at the same altitude until the symptoms disappear. If they do not, however, you should retreat to a lower altitude. Some people are more susceptible than others and learn that there is a limit to the altitude that they can comfortably reach.

If you continue to go higher without acclimatizing and symptoms persist, the condition is likely to become worse. Therefore, don't push forward; head back down to a safer altitude.

Acute Mountain Sickness (AMS) is often lumped together with altitude sickness, but is now believed to be different. While the symptoms of altitude sickness are a result of oxygen starvation, AMS shows up later and appears to be a result of the effects of altitude sickness.

Pulmonary edema — where the lungs fill with fluid and lung tissue swells — is one possible aspect of AMS. This is uncommon below 12,000 feet. Cerebral edema — swelling of the brain tissue — usually occurs at higher altitudes, over 14,000 feet. AMS is noted for severe flu-like symptoms, hacking dry cough, disorientation, confusion and lack of coordination, partial paralysis, and severe respiratory distress.

An avalanche in progress. While you can learn to recognize avalanche-prone terrain, no one can accurately predict when one will occur.

to avoid it. There are two reasons that we are more susceptible to sun in the winter: glare and elevation. Ultraviolet rays are reflected, rather than absorbed, by the snow-covered ground, effectively giving them a second "shot" at your eyes. Additionally, the thinner air in the mountains absorbs less solar radiation, so the sun is "stronger."

Quality sunglasses are the answer, and ideally should block close to 100% of ultraviolet A, B, and C rays (UVA, UVB and UVC). Since reflected sun is such a problem, it is a good idea to purchase large, close-fitting lenses that have leather or rubber around the sides to prevent light from entering under the lens. Mountaineering glasses, such as Julbos, are your best bet.

The treatment for AMS is a rapid descent to lower altitude.

SNOW BLINDNESS

Snow blindness is actually sunburn of the eyes, and that painful description alone should be adequate reason

SUNBURN AND WINDBURN

For the same reasons that snowblindness is likely in winter, sunburn is also a threat. Fortunately, most of your skin is covered in winter, so your main concerns are your cerns are your

A probe pole can be useful in pinpointing the location of an avalanche victim, but it is no substitute for a transceiver.

face and ears. Take the same precautions that you would in tropical areas: liberally apply sunblock with a high Sun Protection Factor (SPF).

Windburn feels similar to mild sunburn, but is an irritation caused by wind moving across the skin. It can be treated or prevented by applying a lubricant such as sunscreen. Some winter skin products are specifically labeled for both sun and wind protection.

AVALANCHES

No word puts more fear in the hearts of winter travelers than "avalanche." The image it conjures up — of massive amounts of snow pouring down a slope, destroying everything in its

path, including trees and buildings — is truly scary. Yet most snowshoers will never encounter such a phenomenon; those who are in areas prone to avalanches can often avoid them.

Surprisingly, the smaller nondestructive avalanches that are over in a matter of seconds are more dangerous to snowshoers than the bigger ones, since they are more frequent, and harder to spot and avoid. Even a small slide can quickly bury a person.

There are two major causes of avalanches. One is when too much snow accumulates on a slope that is too steep to hold it, and, thus, ends up sliding off. This type of

Quality sunglasses that block close to 100% of ultraviolet A, B, and C rays are a must to prevent painful snow blindness.

In avalanche country all members of a party should wear an avalanche transceiver, a small radio that sends and receives signals, allowing rescuers to locate buried victims quickly.

avalanche tends to be less severe, since there is a limit to the amount of snow the slope will hold, and often the result is just a repositioning of the snow to the base of the slope, rather than a full-fledged avalanche. It is easy to spot very steep slopes where this is likely to occur.

Less steep slopes — under 45 degrees — are actually prone to the more dangerous type of avalanches, and can be much more difficult to spot. Avalanches that occur on these slopes are caused by weak bonds between layers of snow, which can be the result of several different factors, including wind, time, temperature, or the formation of ice crystals.

When there has been no snowfall for a while, time consolidates the existing snow into a firm pack. Then when a lot of new fresh snow falls, you really have two layers of snow with different densities. An avalanche occurs when the upper layer slides on the lower layer. The cause can be movement, from a snowshoer or skier; a change in temperature causing the upper layer to begin to melt; or just gravity and an over accumulation of snow.

ACCLIMATIZING ON EVEREST

The need to allow the body to acclimate to high elevations is one reason that climbing Mount Everest has taken on the legendary proportions it has. It is far from the most technically demanding climb, as evidenced by the novice adventurers who have been led up to the summit by guides. But the feat requires time, usually four to eight weeks. Typically five camps are made at progressively higher altitudes. Climbers go slightly higher each day and then return to camp at night to allow their bodies to recover. In this fashion, they slowly advance toward the summit. Once they push above 25,000 feet, they have entered into what even the most experienced climbers refer to as "the death zone."

Avalanches are most likely to occur during or immediately after storms, especially when large amounts of snow are deposited in a short time period. Fortunately, most snowshoers stay out of the high peaks during severe winter storms. Another prime time for avalanches is when a long cold spell is followed by a period of rapid warming. As upper layers begin to melt, moisture forms between layers, lowering the friction and making it easier for the upper layers to slide.

Avalanches often occur in the same places year after year, and in some national parks or forests avalanche warnings may be posted. Telltale signs of avalanche-prone areas include strips devoid of trees and steep narrow chutes. If you are snowshoeing, even on level ground, and your footsteps make a loud hollow noise, or the surface around your steps splinters and cracks, the snow in the area is probably unstable, and all slopes in that area should be avoided.

If you need to traverse slopes in questionable areas, go one at time, with your partners observing the uphill side of the slope. Undo your backpack straps before crossing, in case you have to drop the backpack quickly. On long trips in avalanche country, snowshoers often carry avalanche transceivers, which help rescuers to locate them. Many also wear avalanche cords, long sec-

This trekking ski pole model converts into a 260-cm avalanche probe, a simple but important rescue tool.

tions of colored rope trailing from their waists, to make their location easier to spot.

If you are traveling in avalanche-prone country — which you should only do with proper training — two other essential items to carry with you are an avalanche probe and shovel. Both of these are to be used in the event that you or one of your companions is buried and needs to be rescued. An avalanche probe is really just a long stick or pole that is used to search the freshly displaced snow for buried victims. Some companies are now making trekking poles that connect to become a longer avalanche probe.

The shovel is used to dig out victims once you find them, either from a search with a probe or by locating their avalanche cord or transceiver signal. Mountaineers usually carry lightweight folding shovels, but in a pinch, many snowshoes can be used for this purpose.

While avalanches can and do occur below treeline and in the woods, it is far safer to be in thick forests than open slopes. If you are traveling in avalanche country and conditions, such as snowfall or sudden warming, indicate possible avalanche activity, it is a good idea to change your route to a lower one in the woods.

FIRST AID KITS

Several outdoor equipment manufacturers offer preassembled first aid kits, which are often comprehensive enough for most purposes, neatly packed, and lightweight. They also sell first aid pouches that you can use to pack and carry your own supplies. The leader in this field is Outdoor Research, who makes an exhaustive selection of specialty kits for different pursuits, including hiking, biking, mountaineering, and whitewater rafting, as well as for general travel.

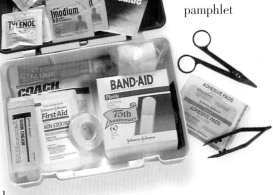

Carrying a first aid kit on all snowshoeing treks is a sound practice. However, a first aid kit is useless without the proper training. Therefore, before venturing out into the wilderness, it is a wise idea to take a first aid course (check with your local Red Cross chapter for course schedules).

If you are putting together your own first aid kit, you should include:
- A variety of bandages (adhesive, ACE, etc.)
- Medical tape
- Antiseptic
- Antibiotic lotion
- Painkillers
- Tweezers
- Scissors
- Useful medications (aspirin, cold and flu, antacids, etc.)
- Blister kit
- SAM splint
- Thermometer
- Instant heat packs
- Safety pins
- First aid book or pamphlet

D R E S S I N G
F O R   W I N T E R

Snowshoeing is a fun, safe sport. The key to your comfort, safety, and enjoyment is dressing properly, which can prevent most of winter's threats, including frostbite, hypothermia, windburn, and general annoyance with the weather (see Chapter 8, Winter Safety).

While there are many innovations that can benefit you, most snowshoers can make do with existing wardrobes, as long as they are used correctly. If money is no object, however, you are lucky indeed, as there has never been a better selection of clothing available for snowshoeing. Outdoor apparel manufacturers have finally addressed the core issue of winter sports attire — breathability — ensuring that those who pursue vigorous outdoor activities in winter no longer have to make trade-offs between comfort and protection. The most important thing to remember when dressing for the outdoors, is to wear several layers (see "ABCs of Layering," page 128).

INNER LAYER

To stay warm in the winter, you have to stay dry. Moisture on the skin leads to evaporative heat loss, and wet clothes against the skin lead to conductive heat loss. Make no mistake about it, staying dry is one of the keys to winter comfort.

Many people think of staying dry in terms of fending off rain and snow, but during highly aerobic activities like snowshoeing, the greatest source of moisture is from within, in the form of perspiration. Ideally, you will adjust your layers to avoid overheating, but even after you have stripped down to next to nothing, you will still sweat during vigorous snowshoeing.

To keep your skin dry, the inner layer must wick or transport moisture away from your skin. Several materials do this job admirably. The industry standard has long been polypropylene (also known as olefin), a quick-drying, hydrophobic syn-

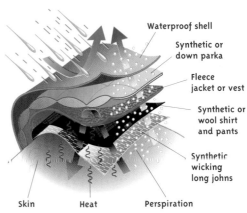

Waterproof shell

Synthetic or down parka

Fleece jacket or vest

Synthetic or wool shirt and pants

Synthetic wicking long johns

Skin   Heat   Perspiration

thetic. Light and inexpensive, it is used in underwear, as well as sock and glove liners.

Newer polyester-based fabrics, such as Patagonia's highly-regarded Capilene, combine layers so that the skin side wicks moisture to an outer surface that spreads it out for faster evaporation. A similar product is

ABCs OF LAYERING

The idea of layering is not new, but it has been refined to a point that blends science and art. When dressing for the outdoors, you can choose from a wide range of materials and styles; as long as you adhere to the basics of layering, you can be comfortable in all weather conditions.

Layering accomplishes several purposes at once. It traps air within the fabrics, as well as between them, creating more air

spaces, and therefore more insulation. Layering also allows flexibility, as it is easy to add or remove a layer to regulate comfort. The idea is to be comfortable at all times, so you might remove a layer while snowshoeing, then put it on again when you stop. Finally, layering helps to keep you dry by controlling moisture.

In the old days, layers were combined into one garment, the parka, which gave you two choices: on or off. Parkas are fine for when you are stationary — sit-

Wearing several layers of clothing is the key to remaining warm and dry in any active winter sport. Even on half-day outings, stuff extra layers, including outer shell jacket and pants, into a day pack.

bipolar fabric from Malden Mills.

There are many other "inner layer" materials produced by rep-utable manufacturers, all of which have wicking properties. Some are made of material that is naturally

---

ting around a campfire or at a football game — but are not well suited to aerobic activities. If you are going to be active, layering is the way to go. There are three basic layers, although you might decide to wear several more.

INNER LAYER

Also known as the skin layer, this is what you wear against your body, and its primary purpose is one of moisture transportation. The idea is to keep your skin as dry as possible, and the inner layer is worn to accomplish this.

MIDDLE LAYER

Known as the insulating layer, this can actually consist of several layers, the purpose being to pro-vide insulation and keep you warm. While you might use the same inner and outer layer all the time, varying your middle layer can enable you to be comfortable in temperatures ranging from mild to bitter cold.

OUTER LAYER

Known as the shell layer, this pro-tects you and the other layers from the elements.

wicking, while others are chemically treated or specially woven to create this effect. The important thing is that they all accomplish the same goal: they keep you dry.

One fact that mountaineers learned long ago is that cotton kills. While cotton is a versatile and comfortable fabric, perfect for regular underwear, sweatshirts or sweatpants, and dress shirts, it is slow to dry, does not wick, and loses almost all of its insulation value when wet. In really cold weather, even a solitary pair of cotton briefs can undermine your attempts to stay warm. Men, in particular, sweat a lot and lose much heat through the area around the groin — one of the most important regions to keep dry. Therefore, the same manufacturers that make wicking long underwear offer boxers

FLEECE, WONDERFUL FLEECE

No material has had as much impact on the world of outdoor clothing as polyester fleece. While clothing manufacturers debate which are the best waterproof shell materials, breathable fabrics, and underwear designs to use, they almost all agree on the use of fleece. Whereas the word fleece once referred to sheepskin, it is now understood to mean a synthetic pile fabric, sometimes made from recycled soda bottles. While companies tout their own brand names, many have their fleece made for them by venerable Malden Mills, creator of the well-known Polartec label. Originally popularized in pullovers by Patagonia, fleece is now used in almost every type of product from almost every garment manufacturer.

Fleece is light, warm, quick drying, and retains most of its insulation value when wet; a great substitute for wool, with which it shares some of these properties. One of the reasons for its popularity is that it is available in a wide range of colors and weights, and is very comfortable against the skin. Below are the popular types of Polartec fleece products and their applications:

● Regular Polartec comes in three weights: 100, 200, and 300 (also known as expedition).

● Series 200 Power Stretch combines Lycra with 200-weight Polartec for a stretch material that can be used to make very warm tights, which can be worn as an inner layer.

● Series 1000 Windbloc adds a windproof barrier and is treated for water resistance, enabling it to be used as an outer layer.

and briefs made of high-tech synthetics.

If you are a cotton lover, all is not lost. Demand for natural fabrics has led manu-facturers to begin working on cotton-based materials with small amounts of synthetics blended in for wicking. While much of this technology is as yet untested, in the future you may be able to purchase cotton underthings, and even denim jeans, that are adapted for the rigors of out-door use.

Different people feel outdoor temperatures differently, as this couple shows: the woman wears her outer shell while the man is down to his fleece vest.

MIDDLE LAYER

The middle layer or layers provide insulation. These are the layers that should be added or removed according to level of activity and weather conditions. For instance, on a mild day, you might just wear a fleece vest over your wicking layer and under your shell. If it's slightly colder, you might wear a fleece pullover; colder yet, you can wear both; even colder, you can add a down vest. Vests are especially versa-tile for layering, as they can be packed into a small space when not in use. When worn, they insulate the body's core, while allowing unre-stricted arm movement.

A synthetic fleece pullover (right) is
a favorite middle-layer insulator,
while a nylon shell outer layer
(below) keeps warmth in and
protects against wind and
wet snow.

Thinsulate, Hollofill,
Lite Loft, Polarguard,
Primaloft, and
Quallofil.

The properties
to look for in the
insulating layer
are light
weight,
breathability,
and comfort.
Since you
want as much
moisture as possible
to escape to the outside, avoid
insulating layers that trap moisture.

No synthetic has yet to match
the cozy comfort of down for its insulating value, but the major drawback
of down is that it becomes nearly
useless when wet. With a protective
shell layer, however, this should not
be a problem. Down is
often used in very cold
situations, and incorpo-
rated into heavy-
duty moun-
taineering
outfits. Other
popular
insulating
materials
include
fleece,
wool, and
synthetic
down sub-
stitutes,
such as

OUTER LAYER

The outer
layer protects
you from wind,
snow, and rain —
but that is easier said
than done. The first big
revolution in winter sports
outerwear came with the
invention of Gore-Tex, a waterproof,
breathable laminate that is applied to
other fabrics. It immediately caught
on among Alpine skiers, who needed
protection from severe weather conditions, yet appreciated the material's
breathable quality.

Since the introduction
of Gore-Tex, many competitors have appeared,
including Sym-
patex, Ultrex,
Triple Point
Ceramic,
H2No, and
MemBrain.
All are
excellent
choices for
back-
packers
and
climbers who
will inevitably

get caught in downpours, and for anyone else who spends long periods in the rain or in frequent contact with the snow, such as snowboarders. They are not good choices, however, for those involved in highly aerobic activities like snowshoeing, running, or cross-country skiing.

The problem is breathability: As a rule, the more waterproof a fabric is, the less breathable. The amount of breathability that these garments provide is nowhere near enough to dispel the perspiration given off by a person engaged in a vigorous sport like snowshoeing. Many of my companions, who are winter sports enthusiasts, have found themselves soaked in sweat and questioning the so-called breathability of their shells that cost several

When it comes to expeditions that take you into high country, there is no substitute for quality clothing. It is worth every penny of added expense.

hundred dollars. It's not that these fabrics don't breathe, they just don't breathe enough. Most snowshoers have no need for waterproof garments. Unless they are on long trips, they rarely snowshoe in the rain, and spend little time in contact with the snow.

Ultra-breathable fabrics like Activent finally address the problem posed by aerobic winter sports: how to dispel wind and rain *and* perspiration.

extremely breathable and also water and wind resistant. The level of water resistance is sufficient to protect the user against snow and light rain, as well as incidental spray and contact from snow on the ground. The wind resistance varies among the fabrics, with some being completely windproof. This is

The outdoor clothing community has finally addressed this issue with several new products that are actually more important than waterproofness, as wind greatly increases heat loss. Best of all, these materials

WHAT IS INSULATION ANYWAY?

All insulating products, from pink fiberglass in your walls to down jackets to igloos, function by trapping air. It is the air itself, not the fiberglass, feathers, or snow, that keeps you warm. The more air that is trapped, the higher the insulation value.

No fabric provides warmth, it merely maintains it. Your body produces heat: insulation limits its escape. When you overheat, it is because there is too much insulation and not enough heat is escaping. When you are cold, there is not enough insulation and too much heat is escaping. But no insulation will manufacture heat for you, which is why placing a

can be as much as five times more breathable than the most breathable of waterproof fabrics.

The most common of these new fabrics is microfiber, which gets its properties from the tightness of its weave. Often made of polyester, microfiber materials are chemically treated for additional water resistance. Popular name brands include Hydrenaline, Pulse, and Clima-FIT.

A new "wonder fabric" from the folks at W.L. Gore is Activent, a highly breathable material that is water resistant and completely windproof. This is perhaps the perfect material for the snowshoer, and what I use for my shell layer.

Besides the material, other features to look for in a shell are a hood, snug closures at the wrists, a storm flap over the zipper to keep wind out, ample pockets that can be used while wearing gloves, and pit-zips. These are zippers located under the armpits

Don't forget that wool is still one of the great breathable insulators, and it's more economical and durable than synthetics.

that can be opened to allow additional moisture to escape in warmer weather or during more vigorous activities.

hypothermic individual in a sleeping bag may have little effect, since he or she will be unable to generate sufficient body heat to allow the insulating properties of the sleeping bag to "do their job."

In addition to the air trapped within the material itself, air trapped between the layers of material also provides insulation. For this reason, two thin layers of down will be warmer than a single layer. The only garments that provide warmth in and of themselves are those with artificial heat sources, such as battery-powered socks. Artificial heat packs, which can be placed inside clothing, are a newer option. To keep warm while camping, some people place warm water bottles inside their sleeping bags.

Minus 30°F in Lolo National Forest, Bitterroot Mountains, Montana. In such cold, a hood and balaclava keep head and face warm. Goggles (below) protect eyes from glare and wind.

because much heat is lost to radiation from the large surface area of the uncovered head. A hat is vital in order to stay warm in cold conditions, and can be the best way to regulate heat. I often remove my hat while snowshoeing, stick it in a pocket, and then replace it when I stop. This one easy change is often all I need to remain comfortable, whether I'm active or inactive.

Hats can also protect vulnerable parts of the head such as ears and cheeks, depending on their design. On mild days, you can often opt for a fleece or wool ear band, which will protect your ears from frostbite but leave your head uncovered. On colder days, you may need both an ear band and hat. Hats also protect your scalp from sunburn, which is especially important at higher altitudes.

For your hands, systems often consist of a polypropylene liner, a fleece glove, and a shell of Gore-Tex or similar material. Some shell gloves are extra long and cover the gap at the wrist; many include a drawstring to ensure a snug fit. Fleece gloves with a wind-blocking layer are becoming popular, since your extremities are especially vulnerable to the effects of wind.

Pay attention to quality construction, especially stitching. Good outerwear has taped seams, with tape applied to the inside of all seams to ensure water and wind resistance. The best waterproof fabrics are useless if the manufacturer leaves holes, such as those around the stitches, untreated.

HEAD, HANDS, AND FEET

There is a saying among outdoor types: "If your feet are cold cover your head." This makes sense,

White Mountains, New Hampshire. With the right clothing (and skills), you can safely experience the pristine beauty of high peaks in winter.

Mittens are definitely warmer than gloves, although there is a trade-off in terms of dexterity.

Socks are the key to keeping your feet warm, dry, and comfortable. Since your feet are farthest from your body's warm core, and your toes have small blood vessels and less circulation, your feet are the hardest part of the body to keep warm.

Do not compound this already-difficult situation by letting them get wet. To keep your feet warm you must keep them dry! This means protecting them not only from outside sources of wetness — like snow — but also from inside sources, like the sweat and condensation that develop inside your boots.

The first defense against moisture is an inner layer of wicking material. The most common choice is polypropylene, but silk is sometimes used, as are a wide array of synthetics. Always use sock wicking liners — not just for when you are snowshoeing, but for when you are involved in any cold-weather activity. They are also great to use during warm-weather sporting activities, such as hiking and biking. At a couple dollars a pair, they are the best investment you can make.

Your main pair of socks should be made of wool, a wool blend, or polyester fleece, but never cotton, which is slow to dry, and loses almost all of its insulating value when wet. One drawback to socks made of fleece is that they are not as form fitting as those made of wool blends and may cause blisters. Fleece can also get packed down with use, which causes it to lose some of its insulation value.

WINTER CAMPING

Winter camping is not a minimalist activity — you can't just sleep beneath the stars by a roaring campfire in your clothes. It requires a great deal of specialized equipment and knowledge.

Many outdoor outfitters and retailers offer courses or classes in winter camping, and there are several excellent books on the subject. Nonetheless, your first trip should be with someone who is an experienced winter camper, whether an acquaintance or a guide. There are many such trips run by trail associations, outing clubs, and outdoor schools every winter (see Sources & Resources).

Winter camping is not for everyone. Many snowshoers enjoy themselves without ever spending a night out of doors, just as many hikers never camp. But for some, winter camping is practical, since it allows them to go farther, climbing peaks or seeing sights that could not be reached in one day. In addition, cabins and campgrounds that are overflowing in summer are often empty in winter. Winter camping can also be a fulfilling and spiritual experience. Hot chocolate can be much more satisfying in a snow cave or tent than in your dining room, and the quiet beauty and wonder of winter become even more apparent

Nightfall on a backcountry tour in the Selkirks, British Columbia, Canada. The warmth of a campfire is especially welcome at 10° below.

to someone who spends both days and nights communing with nature.

First-timers should spend only one night outdoors. You should plan your trip so that you remain fairly close to civilization, and use a man-made shelter. If you find that spending a winter's night in a cabin is not comfortable for you, then you can be relatively sure that you will not enjoy sleeping out in a tent. This is not only a safer approach, but a more cost-effective one as well. Quality four-season tents cost hundreds of dollars, so it makes sense to find out whether you enjoy winter camping before taking the plunge.

GEAR

When packing for a winter camping trip, the natural tendency is to bring everything. Unfortunately, this strategy is not far from actuality. In the winter, you need to bring a lot more gear than you would for an equivalent trip in the summer.

Clothing

Clothing is the first order of business. In addition to all your layers, you will need extra, dry inner layers for the additional days. Wet clothing does not dry overnight in winter; socks and underwear can be dried using body heat by sticking them in your sleeping bag, but this is not very comfortable, and does not always work. Besides, you may have to keep your water in there to prevent it from freezing.

It is also a good idea to bring additional heavier clothing to wear at camp. You will be much colder at the camp than you were getting there, because you are no longer active, and the temperature drops significantly at night. The lightweight hiking boots and wool socks that kept you warm while snowshoeing will not protect your feet while sitting in the snow. Plan on carrying down booties and a light down jacket or sweater.

Summer backpackers often live by the rule of leaving anything home that they do not expect to need. The opposite is true in winter. Bring anything you think you might need. This includes extra gloves, an extra hat, sock liners, and anything else that might get wet or lost that you cannot proceed without. Redundancy might make life harder on your back, but the winter is awfully unforgiving.

Sleeping Bags

Whether you spend the night in a cabin, tent, or snow cave, the sleeping bag is your primary protection and shelter. A bulky, cotton, roll-style bag like you used during your Scout Troop days is not the way you want to go for your first line of defense against the elements.

When you go to look at sleeping bags, there will be two types: three season and four season. The first type

First-timers ought to spend only one night out and remain close to civilization. The additional gear, clothing, and food winter demands will weigh you down plenty, even on an overnight.

is just what it says, and not good for winter camping. The latter type is somewhat deceiving, as these bags are only good for cold weather. If you plan on doing much winter camping, take the plunge and invest in a cold-weather bag. However, if you will be using your sleeping bag year-round, the best way to go is to buy a quality, low-rated, three-season bag, and upgrade it for winter use (see "Increase the Warmth of Your Sleeping Bag," page 143).

SHAPE AND SIZE If you have decided to buy a four-season bag, you will not have much choice when it comes to shape, as almost every cold-weather bag is a mummy, the most efficient shape for both weight and body-heat

Mummy bags are the warmest, but some find tight-fitting ones constrictive. Try various models on for size before buying.

retention. For comfort, three-season bags are often more rectangular in shape, however, it is best to stick to the mummy design.

Sleeping bags usually come in regular and long sizes, and include height rating. These ratings are very conservative, so if you are "borderline," opt for the larger bag. A minor increase in weight and space in your pack will be offset by increased comfort. In addition, you may have to stick items such as drinking water and damp clothing inside your bag to keep them from freezing, and will, therefore, appreciate the extra room.

A hood that tightens around your head and shoulders is an important feature for winter camping, and many sleeping bags offer a draft collar to close off the opening at the head.

INSULATION There are two choices of insulation — down and synthetic. By weight, down is the best insulator, and down sleeping bags compact extremely well. But down has to be kept dry to work, which is not always easy in winter. If you are

Square-box baffle construction (bottom) provides maximum loft and warmth. Offset quilted batts (top) and slant-box baffles (middle) also are effective.

going to be camping in huts, down bags are an excellent choice, but if you are planning to sleep in snow caves, synthetics are probably better.

The leading synthetic bag insulations are Lite Loft and Polarguard. While you sacrifice some weight and size, these materials will keep you warm even in moist conditions.

The insulation in sleeping bags is contained in baffles, which are tubes sewn across the bag. There are many different ways to make baffles, and better bags use more efficient

Cutaway view of down-filled bag shows how baffles keep down from shifting.

designs, including overlapping baffles and an extra baffle behind the zipper. The idea is to protect and insulate the bag at points where there would otherwise be no insulation, such as around seams.

Whether you get a down or synthetic bag, do not store it in the stuff sack provided. This is designed to compress the bag as much as possible to save room on your camping trip; using it for larger storage may permanently affect the loft and there-

INCREASE THE WARMTH OF YOUR SLEEPING BAG

Winter comfort does not end with your sleeping bag. There are several ways you can increase the warmth of your sleeping bag, or even turn a three-season bag into a four-season model.

The first and easiest way to increase warmth is to leave some clothes on when you get into your sleeping bag. The same layering principles that work for your clothing during the day also work

at night. So wear fleece pants and a pullover to bed. Don't forget to wear socks or booties, gloves, and a hat to sleep, since protecting your hands, feet, and head is also very important. If you are still not warm enough, keep putting on more clothes until you are comfortable, as long as they are dry. Never wear wet clothing to bed.

There are three sleeping bag accessories that can increase its warmth. One is a bag cover, a zip-

continued on page 144

pered cover that goes over your bag, and traps a layer of air, thus increasing insulation and reducing conductive heat loss to the air and ground.

There are also sleeping bag liners, which are lightweight and often made of fleece. Liners can add as much as 15 degrees of comfort to your bag, can be used alone in summer, and are also good for just sitting around in a cold cabin. An added benefit is that they are much easier to wash and keep clean than the inside of your sleeping bag.

The last accessory that you can use is an insulated pad. This is of tremendous importance whenever you are sleeping on a cold surface, whether it be the snow or the floor of a tent or cabin. To reduce conductive heat loss, you need a full-length sleeping bag pad, either of thick foam or an inflatable style insulated with air. Many lightweight summer campers make do with a three-quarter-length pad of thin foam. However, this will not be sufficient in winter.

Todd Alexander, longtime snowshoer and winter camper, has his own solution. Since he owns a lightweight, high-quality three-season bag, and an ultralight summer down bag for bicycle touring, he chose not to invest in a winter bag. "I just bring both my bags, which do not weigh much more than a cold weather bag, and I put one inside the other."

fore insulation value of your bag. Store the bag in an uncrowded manner that allows it to breathe, such as in an old pillowcase. When you do go winter camping, remove your sleeping bag from the stuff sack as soon as you make camp, since it will need some time to decompress.
SHELLS AND LINERS W. L. Gore, the supplier that dominates the clothing market with Gore-Tex and Activent, also makes the most desirable sleeping bag shell material, DryLoft.

A windproof, water-resistant, and highly breathable fabric, DryLoft is used in the most expensive sleeping bags. A similar, but slightly less expensive choice, is microfiber. Most other bags have shells of nylon, a breathable but less moisture-resistant material.

The sleeping bag lining functions just like the inner layer of your clothing, and should be made of a comfortable wicking material. Most bags are lined with a nylon taffeta, and some models use a material called Thermastat.

Tents

Tents suitable for winter camping are described by manufacturers as four-season models, although it's unlikely you would want to lug around the weight of one of these sturdy models in the summer.

Four-season tents seam-sealed against melting snow and equipped with vestibules to hold extra gear make for cozy winter accommodations.

Four-season tents are made of heavier material with beefier poles, in shapes especially designed to withstand vigorous winds and the weight of snow. The floors usually wrap around and come up higher on the walls than summer tents. This is known as a "bathtub" design, and it helps to keep water out. Since these tents are more resistant to the elements, they are also less breathable, and tend to accumulate condensation inside.

The North Face VE-25 four-season mountaineering tent (with rain fly) sleeps four.

A new trend in four-season tents is single-wall construction, where one layer of heavier waterproof material replaces the traditional two-layer shell and fly construction. These tents are lighter and quicker to pitch, but the trade-off is reduced ventilation and breathability.

Even the most waterproof of tents should be seam-sealed before use, and regularly thereafter. This is a simple but important job, as the seams are the weak link in any waterproof garment, tent, or fabric. A tube of seam-sealer costs a couple of dollars, and is easily applied to the inside of the seams.

Most high-quality tents (and there are no others for winter camping) have matching vestibules, and the increased weight is usually worth the added space. A vestibule is like a front porch for a tent — a small extension that goes over the entrance and increases the interior square footage, sometimes by nearly 50 percent.

In winter, you have so much gear that needs protection from the elements that it usually will not fit in the tent with you. For instance, in the summer, unless there is a serious threat of rain, I never take my pack into the tent. In the winter, I do. If you are with one or two companions, imagine the space required for three packs, three pairs of boots, three sets of drying clothes, and so on.

The vestibule is also where you will cook in those dire circumstances when you are forced to do this chore inside. Additionally, it is where you can hang clothes, or just spread things out a little bit. Tents are never roomy, so the extra space comes in handy, and makes a vestibule a worthwhile investment.

Food

You will also need to bring more food in winter than summer, since this is the fuel your body uses to generate heat. Poor diet is one of the contributing factors to hypothermia. Bring foods that can be eaten uncooked, such as cheese, crackers, and jerky, as well as ready-to-cook dishes, such as pasta. Freeze-dried backpackers' meals are not exceptionally tasty, but many winter campers find themselves fairly uninterested in preparing an extensive dinner. Look for lightweight foods that pack plenty of carbohydrates, and don't worry about limiting your fat intake in winter. You can theoretically make do without hot food, although it is not pleasant, and since you will need to melt snow for drinking water anyway, you might as well enjoy some hot soup or stew.

Stove

To prepare food and melt snow for drinking water, you will need a good stove. As with every other piece of outdoor equipment, it is important to read the directions, and assemble, and test out your stove before leaving home. Even if you are experienced with your stove, you may find it much more difficult to start and operate in cold or windy environments. Take along waterproof matches as a backup, but don't plan on making a campfire, since dry wood is understandably scarce in deep snow.

If you tent camp, you will need a platform to support your stove while cooking, or it will melt a hole in the snow and disappear, an event that will be humorous only much later. A piece of foam cut from a sleeping pad works well, and has numerous other uses, such as a seat on the snow or for protecting stoves and photographic equipment.

There are several types of stove fuels on the market. For winter snowshoe camping, white gas is best. It

A kitchen counter carved in snow. A platform to support your stove will keep it from melting a hole in the snow and disappearing.

burns at low temperatures, generates the highest temperatures, and burns cleanly, with no odor or smoke. In general, you should avoid using a stove in your tent, but in winter you sometimes have no choice, so you will appreciate the absence of a gas smell.

The snow cave can provide snug, relatively spacious living quarters when snow conditions are right and you're planning to stay put for several days.

The only downside of white-gas stoves is that they require priming.

Although propane also works well in low temperatures, the fuel needs to be carried in heavy metal bottles, and winter campers have enough weight to deal with already. White gas can be carried in much lighter bottles, so opt for stoves that burn this substance.

Bring more fuel in winter than you would in summer. You will need plenty of drinking water, and melting snow for water or for cooking requires a lot more energy than bringing room temperature water to a boil, the normal use of camping stoves.

Everything Else

The list of stuff you should bring goes on and on. A first aid kit is a must, and companies like Outdoor Research make excellent ones for camping use. You may save some money by assembling your own, but these kits pack a lot of necessities into a small light package, and often include items you might not think of (see Chapter 8, page 126 for more information).

A first aid kit for your equipment is also necessary, especially for your snowshoes. If you experience a breakdown in your shoes, walking home will become much more difficult (see Chapter 2, page 45, for more information).

Bringing along a map and navigation tools is also important (see Chapter 7). If using a GPS receiver, keep it inside your clothing to preserve battery life, and bring extra batteries. The same goes for your flashlight, which is a real necessity. Many winter campers bring headlamps, which work great in tents or cabins, and are indispensable if you get caught outdoors in the dark. Keep the battery pack inside your jacket.

It gets dark early in winter, and you will probably not be ready to go to sleep at 6:00 o'clock p.m., so you will need both light and entertainment. Candles or a candle lantern offer the most light for the least weight, but make sure you do not set fire to your tent. And throwing a deck of cards into your pack goes a long way toward alleviating cabin fever.

One other item that can be useful and help conserve fuel is a dark-colored water bottle. I use a widemouthed Nalgene quart jar, which is easy to pack with snow. As soon as I reach camp, I fill it up and set it out in the sun, preferably on a rock or piece of wood rather than in the snow. The dark color absorbs sunlight and speeds up the melting process, and often by dinnertime you have a jar of water. Even if it is too cold out for the snow to fully melt, the contents of the jar require less energy to convert to water than snow scooped off of the ground. Just

Everything else you need to bring along winter camping includes a first aid kit, map and compass, candles (more light for their weight than flashlights), and, for some, skis or a snowboard.

remember not to leave the jar out after dark, or it will refreeze.

SHELTERS

There are three types of shelters that are used in winter camping: existing man-made buildings, tents, and snow shelters. Hard-core winter campers may opt to forego shelter altogether and sleep out in the snow in a bivouac sack — especially on mountaineering expeditions — but this is more a matter of necessity than enjoyment. Do not attempt to sleep in the snow unless you have a great deal of winter camping experience.

Cabins and Lean-Tos

Man-made shelters can take the form of cabins or lean-tos. The benefits of both are that they provide protection from the wind, snow, and rain, and get you off of the cold ground. It is also easier to cook, change, and spread out gear in a man-made shelter.

Despite the security of being completely enclosed, cabins do not really offer a pronounced advantage over lean-tos, as they are usually poorly insulated and without a heat source. In other words, it will be just as cold inside the cabin as out, minus the significant windchill. If you do a lot of cooking or are part of a large group, you may be able to raise the interior temperature of the cabin slightly. On the other hand, the lean-to may afford you the option of having a roaring fire in front of the opening, providing light, some heat (though not much), and ambiance.

Some cabins have mattresses, which help to keep you warm and eliminate the need for a sleeping pad. By not having to carry a pad or a tent, you can save some noticeable pack weight.

Tents

Moving from shelters to tents is a major step in winter camping, in terms of experience, comfort, weight, and cost. A high-quality four-season tent like the North Face VE-25 can weigh close to 10 pounds and cost twice as much as a high-quality three-season model. Once you have adapted to winter tent camping, however, there is no limitation to where your snowshoes can take you.

Tents are best pitched on flat, firm surfaces and snowshoes make finding such a spot easy in winter. Simply walk around in circles, stomping down the snow until the right grade and consistency of a snow platform is created.

In very cold weather, climbers often use the excellent insulating properties of snow to their advantage by surrounding the tent with snow to create a hybrid tent/snow shelter. One way to accomplish this is to use a shovel to build a wall of snow around the base of the tent, to a height of two to four feet. The snow wall serves a dual purpose: it blocks wind and insulates the tent walls.

Sometimes in light, deep snow, an easier alternative is to dig out a hole to put the tent in. This can sometimes be achieved by stomping an area equal to the surface area of the tent, especially if you can stomp down to a depth of two feet or more. Otherwise you can actually dig out an impression, with either a shovel or snowshoes, and drop the tent into the hole.

Remember that even with the heaviest of tents, one of your main insulation concerns will be conductive heat loss through the floor. A sleeping bag pad is essential for winter tent camping, and every additional bit of insulation helps, even if you have to improvise by lying on dirty laundry.

The quinzhee (left) is an easily-constructed Native American shelter made by shoveling snow into a mound, then tunneling in. Snow is a better insulator than nylon, though a tent is another option.

Snow Shelters

Snow shelters are not a viable option for beginner winter camping. Although experienced shelter builders can construct a protective structure in less than an hour, it can be a slow, frustrating experience for the uninitiated. Take a course, read a book, and above all, practice by building a shelter in your backyard before you set out. Imagine what could happen if you got into the woods and discovered that you were simply incapable of enclosing a shelter.

Well-made snow shelters can provide a lot of protection from the elements, especially from the cold. These are probably the easiest shelters to warm, even more so than a cabin. Snow is an excellent insulator and traps a lot of air pockets, allowing your body heat to quickly bring the interior temperature well above that of the outside.

One drawback is that it is hard to anticipate the amount and type of snow where you are going. Another is that while you can pitch a tent in minutes, and then begin to change, cook, and relax; building a snow shelter can take three or more hours, greatly reducing the amount of time you have for daylight travel. Usually snow shelters are efficient choices only for stays of more than one night.

Snow shelters can also, at times, be dangerous; there is always the possibility of collapse. A poorly made snow cave can result in being buried alive, an unpleasant and potentially life-threatening experience.

There are three primary types of snow shelters: caves, igloos, and quinzhees. Caves are often the easiest, especially when you have good snow conditions and a gentle slope. Generally the principle is to dig a hole down to a sufficient depth (at least six feet) and then tunnel in horizontally from the bottom of the hole. Obviously, the snow has to be deep, and you will find that it is a lot of work getting the snow you are digging out and to the surface. Building the cave on a slope is easier, since it reduces the depth you need to dig.

Igloos are very efficient structures, and with experience, are fairly easy to build. Without practice, however, they can be downright impossible. Igloos are also fickle, requiring snow conditions that are conducive to forming tightly packed blocks of snow. Eskimos have the benefit of readily available slabs of wind-packed snow, but in many parts of the country good igloo snow is hard to find.

The quinzhee, a native American version of the igloo, is easier to make. The structure is like an above-ground snow cave, and is constructed by first making a big mound of snow, at least six feet high, and even bigger in diameter, using snowshoes and shovels. After packing down the exterior with your hands and snowshoes, you wait for up to two hours as the snow settles and becomes packed into a more solid mass. Once this occurs, you simply dig an entrance and hollow out the interior. Usually a trench is dug to the "door" so that the opening is below surface level and therefore sheltered from incoming wind.

In any snow shelter you should pack the inside surface smooth to minimize dripping from melting snow. Adequate ventilation is also very important, and often vent holes need to be dug through the walls, which should be at least a foot and a half thick. In both igloos and quinzhees, the roof must be somewhat thinner to prevent collapse.

Winter camping is a fun and rewarding experience, but requires a substantial amount of knowledge, equipment, and planning. The best way to learn is to accompany an outfitter, guide, or friend who can supply both experience and gear.

SOURCES & RESOURCES

ORGANIZATIONS

THE UNITED STATES SNOWSHOE ASSOCIATION
Route 25, Box 94
Corinth, NY 12822
Attn.: Candace Bowen-Brown

CANADIAN SNOWSHOE ASSOCIATION
9 Beriault
Hull, Quebec J8X 1A1
Canada

OUTING CLUBS & WINTER CAMPING GROUPS

ADIRONDACK MOUNTAIN CLUB
R.R. 3, P.O. Box 3055
Lake George, NY 12845
518-668-4447
Offers classes, books, trails, and shelters throughout the Northeast.

AMERICAN HIKING SOCIETY
P.O. Box 20160
Washington, DC 20041-2160
703-255-9304
Can recommend outing or hiking clubs in your area, and oversees National Winter Trails Day in February.

APPALACHIAN MOUNTAIN CLUB
5 Joy Street
Boston, MA 02108
617-523-0636
Oversees Appalachian Trail, runs events, and publishes guide books.

COLORADO MOUNTAIN CLUB
710 10th Street
Golden, CO 80401
303-654-2663

GREEN MOUNTAIN CLUB
R.R.1, Box 650
Waterbury Center, VT 05677
802-244-7037
Offers classes, books, trails, and shelters throughout Vermont.

MOUNTAINEERS
300 3rd Avenue West
Seattle, WA 98119
206-284-6310
Offers excellent books on outdoor recreation and winter camping, as well as detailed trail guides. Operates classes and trips throughout the Pacific Northwest.

OUTDOOR SCHOOLS & CLASSES

AMERICAN ALPINE INSTITUTE
1515 12th Street
Bellingham, WA 98225
360-671-1505
Comprehensive training center for climbing and skiing. Offers

courses in mountaineering, ice climbing and expeditioning, survival, and wilderness first aid.

BOULDER OUTDOOR SURVIVAL SCHOOL
Box 1590-M
Boulder, CO 80306
800-335-7404
Offers a variety of courses in summer and winter backcountry skills,

EXUM MOUNTAIN GUIDES
P.O. Box 56
Moose, WY 83012
307-733-2297
Offers climbing and winter travel instruction.

EASTERN MOUNTAIN SPORTS CLIMBING SCHOOL
P.O. Box 514
North Conway, NH 03860
603-356-5433
Operated by national retailer EMS, this school offers single- and multi-day courses in winter safety, climbing, mountaineering, and related topics.

INTERNATIONAL MOUNTAIN EQUIPMENT
P.O. Box 494
North Conway, NH 03860
603-356-7013
Well-regarded climbing school that offers a variety of winter-related courses.

NATIONAL OUTDOOR LEADERSHIP SCHOOL (NOLS)
P.O. Box AA
Lander, WY 82520
307-332-9673
Offers courses and trains future guides, year-round, even for college credit, all over the world.

OUTWARD BOUND
Route 2, Box 280
Garrison, NY 10524
800-243-8520
Offers a wide variety of summer and winter classes and trips.

FIRST AID TRAINING
AMERICAN RED CROSS NATIONAL HEADQUARTERS
431 18th Street, NW
Washington, DC 20006
202-737-8300
Call for information on first aid and CPR classes offered by local chapters.

STONEHEARTH OPEN LEARNING OPPORTUNITIES (SOLO)
P.O. Box 3150
Conway, NH 03818
603-447-6711
Minimum age is 18.

WILDERNESS MEDICAL ASSOCIATES
189 Dudley Road
Bryant Pond, ME 04219
800-742-2931
Offers a variety of courses; minimum age is 16.

WILDERNESS MEDICINE INSTITUTE
P.O. Box 9
Pitkin, CO 81241-0009
970-641-3572
In addition to varied courses offerings, the Institute is a source for backcountry first aid supplies and a variety of books on the subject, including several by executive director and founder Buck Tilton.

THE INTERNET
Trail surfing? Tune in to http://www.trailside.com on the web and find the answers to all your Trailside questions. Where are the greatest bike trails? What brand is that lightweight folding kayak? What's the recipe for the Outback Oven Redwood Pizza? In addition to detailed descriptions of all the Trailside TV episodes—78 in all—click through to the experts, locations, maps, and gear you need to make your own adventure. Check out our sponsors and take a virtual tour

inside Chevy Tahoe. Register to be a guest on the series to tell us about your favorite adventure. Best of all, qualify to win gifts each week at the home of adventure.

Whether you're a hiker, biker, canoeist, or snowshoer, another good place to explore is GORP, the Great Outdoor Recreations Pages (http://www.gorp.com), full of information on gear, books, attractions, feature articles, and links to other web sites of interest.

Also check out the Backcountry Home Page (http://io. datasys.swri.edu/overview.html), with information on hiking clubs, trip reports, gear reviews, weather information, state maps, photos, and hiking wisdom.

VIDEOS
Our own Trailside series of videos that aired on public television are the best inspiration we can offer, including tips and techniques from experts. Several programs focus on or feature snowshoeing: Winter Camping in Montana, Winter Camping in Yellowstone Park, Snowboarding Utah's Wasatch Range, Winter Adventure in Southern Utah's Canyon Country. All are $19.95. Call for a catalog or order by calling 800-TRAILSIDE (800-872-4574) or for information on how to receive a free Trailside book or video and discounts on outdoor gear and travel, call the Trailside Nature Club at 1-888-872-4528.

MAGAZINES
THE SNOWSHOER
P.O. Box 458
Washburn, WI 54891
715-373-5556
Magazine devoted to snowshoeing. Published five times per year; subscription fee of $10.00.

MAIL-ORDER SOURCES OF BOOKS & VIDEOS

ADVENTUROUS TRAVELER BOOKSTORE
P.O. Box 577
Hinesburg, VT 05461
800-282-3963 or 802-482-3330
Fax: 800-282-3963 or
802-482-3546
E-mail: books@atbook.com
Home page:
http://www.gorp.com/atbook.htm
Full selection of more than 3,000 titles. Largest supplier of worldwide adventure travel books and maps.

BACKCOUNTRY BOOKSTORE
P.O. Box 6235
Lynnwood, WA 90836-0235
206-290-7652

VIDEO ACTION SPORTS, INC.
200 Suburban Road, Suite E
San Luis Obispo, CA 93401
800-727-6689 or 805-543-4812
Fax: 805-541-8544
Catalog available.

WILDERNESS ADVENTURES
Box 1410
Bozeman, MT 59771
406-763-4900

MAIL-ORDER SOUCES OF EQUIPMENT

CAMPMOR
P.O. Box 700-B
Saddle River, NJ 07458
800-CAMPMOR
Mail-order retailer with huge selection of tents, sleeping bags, clothing, footwear, snowshoes, and equipment at discounted prices.

CLIMB HIGH
1861 Shelburne Road
Shelburne, VT 05842
802-985-5056
Retailer of their own lines and other brands of climbing and winter sports equipment and clothing.

EASTERN MOUNTAIN SPORTS (EMS)
1 Vose Farm Road
Peterborough, NH 03458
603-924-6154
National retailer of their own brands and other top-quality gear, including tents, clothing, sleeping bags, footwear, snowshoes, and other outdoor equipment. Stores in all major cities.

L.L. BEAN
Freeport, ME 04033
800-221-4221
Venerable catalog dealer of a wide assortment of outdoor equipment and clothing, with unique store open 24 hours.

RECREATIONAL EQUIPMENT INC. (REI)
1700 45th Street East
Sumner, WA 98390
800-426-4840
National retailer and catalog merchant that offers their own label and other top-quality makers of tents, clothing, sleeping bags, footwear, snowshoes, and other outdoor equipment. Co-op with 10% discount to members. Also has travel department that offers trips.

SNOWSHOE MANUFACTURERS

ATLAS SNOWSHOE COMPANY
1830 Harrison Street
San Francisco, CA 94103
800-645-SHOE
Large manufacturer that offers full line of aluminum shoes for recreation, backcountry, and racing, as well as accessories.

ELFMAN SNOWSHOES
245 Tank Farm Road, Unit K
San Luis Obispo, CA 93401
805-543-2822
Offers several styles of folding aluminum snowshoes.

GOOD THUNDER SNOWSHOES
3945 Aldrich Avenue South
Minneapolis, MN 55409
612-824-2385
Manufactures a wide variety of aluminum shoes, including ultralight racers.

HAVLICK SNOWSHOE CO.
2513 State Highway 30
Mayfield, NY 12117
518-661-6447
Manufacturers of a wide range of aluminum and wooden snowshoes.

IVERSON SNOWSHOE COMPANY
P.O. Box 85
Shingleton, MI 49884
906-452-6370
Manufacturer of a wide selection of traditional wooden shoes. Also produces a line of wooden snowshoe furniture.

LITTLE BEAR SNOWSHOES
Spring Brook Manufacturing
2477 I Road
Grand Junction, CO 81505
970-241-0160
Manufacturers of molded plastic snowshoes for children and adults, with a variety of bindings.

NORTHERN LITES
1300 Cleveland
Wausau, WI 54401
800-360-LITE
Manufacturers of ultralight aluminum shoes for recreation, backcountry, and racing.

POWDER WINGS
P.O. Box 3100
Springville, UT 84663
800-453-1192
Manufacturers of shock-corded aluminum folding snowshoes.

RAMER PRODUCTS, LTD.
1803 South Foothills Highway
Boulder, CO 80303
303-499-4466
Manufacturers of all-aluminum (including decking) snowshoes and other aluminum products.

REDFEATHER SNOWSHOES
1280 Ute Avenue #20
Aspen, CO 81611
800-525-0081
Large manufacturer that offers full line of aluminum shoes for recreation, backcountry, and racing, as well as accessories.

ROMP SNOWSHOES
121 South Robinson
Florence, CO 81226
719-784-3292
Manufacturers of both aluminum and all-plastic snowshoes.

SHERPA SNOWSHOE COMPANY
444 South Pine Street
Burlington, WI 53105
800-621-2277
Large manufacturer that offers full line of aluminum shoes for recreation, backcountry, and racing, as well as accessories. Also manufacturers less-expensive brand—Indian Summer.

TECHNIQUE SPORT LOISIR (TSL) SNOWSHOES
P.O. Box 19754
Portland, OR 97280-0754
800-505-3365
Largest European snowshoe manufacturer, now offers full line of all plastic snowshoes with a variety of bindings.

TUBBS SNOWSHOE COMPANY
52 River Road
P.O. Box 207
Stowe, VT 05672
800-882-2748
Largest U.S. manufacturer, offers full line of aluminum and wooden shoes for recreation, backcountry, and racing, as well as accessories.

URSUS OUTDOOR EQUIPMENT
2019 East 7th Avenue
Vancouver, British Columbia
V5N 1S5
Canada
604-254-4517
Offers several aluminum models, specializing in crampon-compatible step-in bindings.

YUBASHOES
2412 J Street
Sacramento, CA 95816
800-598-YUBA
Large manufacturer that offers full line of aluminum shoes for recreation, backcountry, and racing, as well as accessories.

SNOWSHOE KITS
WILCOX & WILLIAMS
6105 Halifax Avenue
Edina, MN 55424
800-216-0710
Offers a variety of do-it-yourself kits for traditional snowshoes and snowshoe furniture. Also sells their kits as assembled shoes.

P H O T O   C R E D I T S

BOB ALLEN PHOTOGRAPHY: 13, 77, 80, 95, 96
ATLAS SNOWSHOE COMPANY: 39
NANCIE BATTAGLIA: 99, 108, 111, 115, 141, 145 (top)
COURTESY L. L. BEAN: 132 (all)
DOUG BERRY/OUTSIDE IMAGES: 37, 40, 43, 76, 121
JAMIE BLOOMQUIST/OUTSIDE IMAGES: 14, 18, 51 (top), 75 (top), 78, 83, 88, 91, 97, 133, 134
PAUL BOISVERT: 103 (top)
DENNIS COELLO: 7, 9, 17, 49, 58, 63, 66, 69, 72, 82 (all), 86, 104, 109, 110, 116, 118, 129
DENNIS CURRAN/COURTESY TUBBS SNOWSHOE COMPANY: 6, 92
BOB FIRTH: 70
GEOFF FOSBROOK/COURTESY TUBBS SNOWSHOE COMPANY: 5 (all), 8 (all), 12 (bottom), 21, 22 (all), 28, 29 (all), 34–35, 36 (all), 38 (all), 41, 42 (left), 44
PAUL GALLAGHER/COURTESY TUBBS SNOWSHOE COMPANY: 24 (left)
JOHN GOODMAN: 46, 47, 51 (bottom), 52, 54 (all), 56 (all), 105?, 113, 125, 126
JOHN GOODMAN/COURTESY CLIMB HIGH: 59, 101, 123 (bottom), 124, 127, 136 (bottom), 138

GREEN MOUNTAIN CLUB, INC.: 11
KENNAN HARVEY: 87 (bottom)
ANDY HENKES: 55
ALAN JAKUBEK: 24 (right), 42 (right), 73, 74, 79
BRIAN LITZ: 60 (all), 123 (top), 151
BECKY LUIGART-STAYNER: 50, 62 (all), 139, 142, 145
HUGHES MARTIN/COURTESY TUBBS SNOWSHOE COMPANY: 10
COLIN MEAGHER/COURTESY TUBBS SNOWSHOE COMPANY: 93, 149
PAT MURI/OUTSIDE IMAGES: 140
TODD POWELL/OUTSIDE IMAGES: 57
PAUL REZENDES: 16
DANIEL R. SMITH: 114
COURTESY TUBBS SNOWSHOE COMPANY: 6, 10, 24 (left), 90, 92, 93, 149
BETH WALD: 87 (top)
DENNIS WELSH: 23, 53, 85, 89, 98, 107, 120, 131, 137
DENNIS WELSH/COURTESY TUBBS SNOWSHOE COMPANY: 90
GORDON WILTSIE: 120, 147, 148
GEORGE WUERTHNER: 12 (top), 31, 48, 102, 135, 135 (top)

INDEX